MW00460345

FROM GRIEF TO LOVE

WALKING AROUND ENGLAND AND WALES

LAURENCE CARTER

Copyright © Laurence Carter 2024

All rights reserved.

No part of this publication may be altered, reproduced, distributed, or transmitted in any form, by any means, including, but not limited to, scanning, duplicating, uploading, hosting, distributing, or reselling, without the express prior written permission of the publisher, except in the case of reasonable quotations in features such as reviews, interviews, and certain other non-commercial uses currently permitted by copyright law.

First published in 2024.
Published by Edward Marmalade Publishing.
ISBN: 978-1-7385315-0-9

Between 1st September 2024 and 31st August 2025, all proceeds from the sale of this product, to a minimum of £10,000, will be given to The Eve Appeal (Reg Charity No. 1091708)

CONTENTS

The Uses of Sorrow ix

Author's Note...xi

Chapter 1 15

Chapter 2 19

Chapter 3 23

Chapter 4 29

The South 33

Chapter 5 35

Chapter 6 41

The Southwest.. 49

Chapter 7 51

Chapter 8 56

Chapter 9 61

Chapter 10 69

Chapter 11 75

Chapter 12 82

Chapter 13 86

Wales.. 95

Chapter 14 97

Chapter 15 102

Chapter 16 116

The Northwest 121

Chapter 17 123

Chapter 18 129

Hadrian's Wall and Northumberland 135

Chapter 19 137

Chapter 20 142

The Northeast 147

Chapter 21 149

Chapter 22 153

Chapter 23 158

Chapter 24 162

Chapter 25 169

The Wash 175

Chapter 26 177

East Anglia 181

Chapter 27 183

Essex and North Kent 187

Chapter 28 189

South Kent and East Sussex 193

Chapter 29 195

Chapter 30 198

Epilogue 201

Acknowledgments 203

Dedicated to Melitta Carter, an extraordinary woman,
who made many lives special.

You would have enjoyed this walk!

THE USES OF SORROW

MARY OLIVER

(In my sleep I dreamed this poem)
Someone I loved once gave me
a box full of darkness.
It took me years to understand
that this, too, was a gift.

AUTHOR'S NOTE

This book contains real names wherever possible. However, throughout the walk, I stayed at bed and breakfasts with hosts – rather than empty properties, as I wanted to socialise – so I have used pseudonyms to protect their privacy. For similar reasons, I have not identified some places where I stayed. The idea of this book only occurred to me three-quarters of the way through the year, so these recollections are subject to the vagaries of memory and best efforts at accuracy. The story follows the chronology of the year, starting in Seaford on England's south coast and venturing clockwise around the English and Welsh coasts, eventually returning to the start.

MAP OF THE WALK JUNE 16, 2018 – JUNE 23, 2019
START AND END: SEAFORD, EAST SUSSEX

CHAPTER 1

BEFORE GRIEF COMES LOVE

"There is never a time or place for true love. It happens accidentally, in a heartbeat, in a single flashing, throbbing moment." — Nancy Mitford

Lilongwe, Malawi, July 1987

You know how they say your life can change in a moment? On a sunny, humid day in July 1987, I walked into a room in the Ministry of Agriculture in the southern African country of Malawi. I was a young transport economist advising the Malawian government on which rural roads to upgrade. I needed data; those roads that connected neighbourhoods growing more food would be prioritised. I strolled into the colonial-era, whitewashed building ringed by hibiscus bushes, the languid, humid warmth of the sunshine accompanying the smiles on the faces of the guards.

In the room, all seemed normal. A lopsided portrait of the president hung on the wall. A gentle breeze blew through the burglar bars, carrying a whiff of the fruit seller's activities outside, perhaps banana or mango. Yellowing reports lay stacked in the corners. I knew from experience that these discarded pages often served as paper cones for little boys selling peanuts in the street.

A young woman stood at the desk, a specialist in agricultural statistics, with dark curly hair, a bright yellow dress, and a beautiful smile. And, as I discovered later, strong opinions and a mean tennis backhand. She gave me the data, but soon our conversation turned to tennis. She and a girlfriend played doubles each week with a couple of guys. One was out of town. Could I join them that evening? That sounded much better than spreadsheeting crop information. They lowered their standards for me, and the four of us enjoyed a game vigorous enough to justify a beer afterwards.

As we dispersed, she asked if I could join a group on a weekend hiking trip. We trekked up Mount Mulanje in southern Malawi, where the rolling mist and waving ferns created an atmospheric, romantic mood. One of us helped the other over a rock; our hands remained clasped afterwards. Two years later, Melitta Alevropoulos and I married.

Looking back on our life together, we had no idea of our luck. We were blessed with three children. We lived in several African countries – Botswana, Malawi, and Swaziland – and the remote South Atlantic island of St. Helena. In 1993 we moved to Washington DC for my work in development.

Then, as the leaves were turning crispy gold and red in the Washington suburbs in October 2012, another life-changing moment occurred. I returned home from work, and Melitta said in a low, worried voice:

"Bad news. The results of my smear test came back. I have cervical cancer. The doctor says I need emergency surgery."

The implications sank in as Melitta talked. I held her hand as she explained that everything depended on whether the doctors had found it early enough. This was my introduction to the tyranny of time around testing for cancer: every week matters. We talked about the practicalities of preparing for the hospital. She fretted about the children. I hugged her to sleep that night, telling her how much I loved her, indeed how we all loved her.

That evening, we told Emily, 22, Nic, 20, and Georgie, 16.

Melitta spent the next few months enduring the trauma of chemotherapy and radiation. The doctors said that perhaps the cancer had not metastasised. We waited for the next MRI, hoping. A few months later, in July 2013, I travelled for my work in development to East Timor, on the opposite side of the world. Engrossed in typing emails, I took a few seconds to pick up the phone. In a small, far-away voice, Melitta said,

"Bad news, the cancer has metastasised; I have 12-18 months left."

I couldn't see her face, hold her hand, or embrace her in a hug. Outside the open shutters, life proliferated. The bright mauve of the bougainvillaea bush, the sickly, sweet fragrance of the frangipani tree, the song of the Timor dusky sparrow...

The call ended. I cried – for Melitta, for the graduations and weddings she would miss, the grandchildren she would never see, our children, and myself.

Two days later I arrived at the hospital, to hold her while she sobbed. I told Melitta that we would find some trials and prove the doctors wrong. I couldn't accept the diagnosis. She was more practical – as she had been throughout our marriage – and began planning.

In June 2014, a year after Melitta's 'no hope' diagnosis, the family travelled to St Andrews in Scotland, for Nic's graduation. Melitta was on a break from radiation and chemotherapy treatment and was strong enough to stroll along the beach, humming the melody from *Chariots of Fire*. She delighted in the crab pools and spotted a common redshank, but mostly watched

Emily, Nic and Georgie enjoying each other's company. We all knew this was her last graduation; she would miss Georgie's ceremony in 2018.

For twenty months Melitta managed through a mix of treatments, bouts of hope, and preparations for the family afterwards. Suddenly, in July 2015, the plunge began; the doctor told us that now he would simply prescribe pain medication. I drove home alone, turned the music up full, shouting, "No, no, no, why…".

Melitta died in early September in our family living room, surrounded by Emily, Nic, Georgie, me, and our two dogs. That morning she had lit up my heart with her smile for the last time. A lock of her dark, curly hair had fallen across her forehead, like on that first day in Lilongwe, Malawi. She was fifty-three years old.

CHAPTER 2

GRIEF

"The worst type of crying wasn't the kind everyone could see – the wailing on street corners, the tearing at clothes. No, the worst kind happened when your soul wept and no matter what you did, there was no way to comfort it." — Katie McGarry

Washington D.C., autumn 2015

The mundane filled the void. Emily, Nic, Georgie and I took the dogs for walks. We had a black and white Shih Tzu, Ella, and a golden-brown standard poodle, Cino. Little and large, bossy, and easy-going. Melitta had trained both well. The four of us would walk slowly, broken, and silent, around the familiar neighbourhood route. Summer's heat and humidity had lingered into early September and the cicadas would announce the onset of evening. Cino kept looking back, searching in vain for his favourite person. We had walked dogs as a family, and Melitta and I as a couple, for over a decade. Now everything had changed.

On our walks a Gladys Knight song kept playing in my mind. When Melitta and I started dating, in the mid-1980s in Malawi, we would often take a picnic into the forest, lie on a blanket, inhaling the aroma of the conifers, and sing along to a cassette of Motown songs, including *It Should Have Been Me*. Now, twenty-eight years later, I wished that she had been the one to survive. I found myself asking the same question several times a week *What would you do, Meloo?* I had ridden on the coattails of her decisiveness for nearly thirty years, and now needed to step up. Nowhere more so than with the children. Melitta had whispered to me several times in the past few weeks: make sure that Emily, Nic and Georgie are OK. They had each been close to Melitta, in the special way of mothers and their children. Emily and Melitta had battled sometimes over the life-stages all first-borns must navigate, both insisting they were right, and bonding again after the storm. Emily matched her mother in sociability and temperament, not to mention dark curls and a love for art. Melitta, who had been the middle child of three sisters, empathized with Nic's frustrations in dealing with his siblings. She fussed over him, insisting he learn the piano and later, when he played, would lie back on the sofa, eyes closed, delighting in the music made by her boy. Towards the end, Nic dug his mother a pond in the garden, a sonata with a spade. Melitta tried to protect Georgie from being teased or ignored by Emily and Nic, and sometimes did not notice when she deliberately provoked her big brother. Fair, unlike her dark-haired siblings, Georgie emulated her mother's kindness and empathy, but with a more placid nature.

I did not know how to assuage their pain. I was especially worried about Georgie, now nineteen, returning alone to university in Manchester, England. We agreed that the four of us would meet up as often as possible, and I scheduled a visit to see Georgie in October. But I knew, deep down, that although we would be there for each other, we would each walk the path of grief in our own way.

For weeks after Melitta passed away, waking up in the morning, half-asleep, I would throw my arm across the bed, ready to snuggle up. A flat, chilly sheet, and an expanse of white emptiness, had replaced the cuddly, warm woman. This sequence would startle me awake, and I would lie still, eyes closed, a tear involuntarily slipping out, adrift in memories, resisting the realities of the day. Cino would only tolerate a few minutes however, before stamping his paws impatiently at the end of the bed. Breakfast trumped mourning.

Life resumed, an empty normal. Emily returned to work in New York, Georgie to university in Manchester and Nic stayed at home with me, as he was working in Washington. The kindnesses and suggestions piled up. Neighbours and friends cooked multiple meals for Nic and me and invited us to their homes. Three people gave me Joan Didion's *The Year of Magical Thinking*. Recommendations flooded in for therapy, meditation, yoga, and walking. In practice, both Nic and I veered towards losing ourselves in exercise. We rode our bikes to work in Washington along the canal, marvelling at the early morning mist hovering over the Potomac River. We trained for a triathlon. On Fridays he and I would have a beer and dinner together.

One day, at work, a few weeks after Melitta had passed away, a colleague asked whether I was ready to start dating again, assuring me that there were many women in their late forties and early fifties looking for men. Especially men who still had their hair and no beer belly, he added, trying to be helpful. I stared at him wordlessly, and walked away, unable to muster any response.

Nights were the worst; memories would intrude into dreams, transform into wakefulness, followed by aching, dry sobs, and eventually I would fall back into a fitful, half-awake sleep, waiting for dawn. I started to write to Melitta in a journal, rehashing a memory, or telling her about the day. It helped a little.

Later that autumn, on a drizzly November day, bereft of sunshine or meaning, I stumbled upon a piece of cloth that

Melitta had always slept with, covering her nose to limit her lifelong asthma. I smelled it, trying to coax her memory back, and stood there, wavering, tears streaming, weighing up giving it to Goodwill. *C'mon Laurence, pull yourself together, for the kids.* I gave it away, apologising to Melitta that evening in my journal. I sensed that I was focusing inwards too much.

As 2017 dawned, fifteen months after Melitta's death, I resolved at midnight to find a unique way to honour her memory. I wanted to respect Melitta's simple credo that we should leave the world a better place.

CHAPTER 3

THE DECISION

"The most difficult thing is the decision to act, the rest is merely tenacity. The fears are paper tigers. You can do anything you decide to do." — Amelia Earhart.

Washington D.C, spring 2017

Six-thirty in the morning had always been my favourite time for strolling the neighbourhood with the dogs. Washington's short spring had burst into life. Azaleas revelled in garish reds, pinks, and whites. Daffodil stems lay collapsed in post-flowering exhaustion, violet irises rose regally, and weeds plotted their takeover. And that's where the idea popped into my mind: why not spend a year walking around Great Britain, Melitta's birthplace, to raise awareness about preventing cervical cancer by promoting screening?

I knew Melitta would have liked the idea. Shortly after we met, when we were courting – that word sounds old-fashioned but right – we hitchhiked and bussed around Malawi for two weeks, discovering the country and each other. Steaming up Lake Malawi on the ancient *Ilala,* crammed with passengers, all selling or eating salted fish, the sunset gracing us. Holding onto the seat of a rickety bus careening down the rain-gullied slopes near the northern lakeside mission town of Nkhotakota. Stumbling upon a pottery in the bush, selling the most delicate bowls. Laughing with glee as we splashed in a stream in the Nyika plateau highlands. Relishing the aroma of conifers, while reading, deep in Malawi's central forests. I began to glean the essence of this woman. Melitta's wicked sense of humour teased me out of being too serious. Her fierce competitiveness – middle-child syndrome, she said – and hunger for reading meant she thrashed me at Scrabble. We played most days during the trip and the only question was how much she would beat me by. Her sociability shone through; we stayed with volunteers in every village, people she had met during the two years she had been in Malawi. A romantic bent – a scribbled note with a short poem – was complemented by practicality – where were the bus tickets? We both felt strongly about how Malawians were suffering under the dictatorship of President Banda. Above all, we walked. So, strolling around England and Wales, where Melitta had grown up . . . she would have approved.

I stomped with excitement on the soft asphalt. This felt like another life-changing moment. The dogs nudged me back to reality as they glanced up, unimpressed. I hurried the hounds home and, scanning Google, I learned of an official English coast path, under construction, around 2,800 miles long, and a completed Wales coast path of 870 miles. If I could average ten miles daily, then I could complete the circuit in a year.

Two days later, the fledgling idea had ratcheted into a firm commitment from which there was no humiliation-free escape. I asked my boss about taking a year of unpaid leave. Her eyes misted over. Of course, she said, and she hoped her husband would do something similar for her in the circumstances.

"Talk to HR. You'll need to find a sponsoring organisation

because we'll have to sign an agreement, so we know that you're doing something."

Any vanities I might have had about being irreplaceable vanished in an instant. I mentioned the idea to my children. Emily and Nic were working in the US, while Georgie was attending university in the UK, in Manchester. The word "crazy" came up, but they were enthusiastic and promised to join for a leg or two. Decision made! It felt suspiciously easy. Still, I reassured myself by recalling that the turning points in my life had all been unplanned. I set myself a year to prepare, aiming to start in June 2018.

I learned how over four thousand people have climbed Mount Everest, and nearly two thousand have braved the cold to swim the English Channel. Hundreds of thousands walk the Camino Way each year, and a thousand hardy types complete the entire 2,200-mile Appalachian Trail in the US each summer. Yet only 100-150 people have ever walked around mainland Britain. I wondered why. There seemed to be a gap in the market for bucket-list ambitions that don't require abnormal fitness levels.

During Thanksgiving 2017, Emily, Nic, Georgie, and I batted around names for the campaign, finally landing on '*3500 to End It*' – as in 3,500 miles to end cervical cancer – and set up a website, www.3500toendit.com. Now, I needed a charity partner. I knew of Jo's Cervical Cancer Trust in the UK, dedicated to eliminating cervical cancer. However, I wanted to raise funds for research into changing behaviour around screening and knew that Jo's focused solely on advice and advocacy. I called a friend.

My friend introduced me to another Jo – Jo Marriott, who ran Cancer Research UK's – CRUK for short – volunteer operations in East Anglia. Jo said that a partnership could work and we started fortnightly calls. Jo listened patiently to my ramblings and kept me focused on logistics. Where would I stay?

What about medical supplies? How would I publicise the effort? I noted each question, knowing that I had not thought through the answers, and assured her that it would all work out.

Shortly afterwards, a work colleague's query forced me to think harder about my purpose.

"How much are you hoping to raise?" she asked. She shook her head in bewilderment at my answer, then said, "Why don't you set aside a third of your salary for three years? Why spend a year walking?"

Her blunt challenge forced me to examine my motives. I knew I would need a reason to slog through a drizzly wind for hours every day in the winter. Honouring Melitta's memory was important. But Melitta was practical, with no tolerance for flim-flam. To pay tribute to her, I would need to make a difference.

I researched cervical cancer and was surprised by what I learned. Unlike most cancers, cervical cancer is caused by a virus, the human papillomavirus (HPV). In 2006 a vaccine was approved against the dangerous HPV types leading to cervical cancer. It had to be administered before the onset of sexual activity. The results astounded public health experts; HPV rates fell by 85-90% among vaccinated young women. Adult women who had not had the benefit of the vaccine needed screening. If vaccination and screening reached certain thresholds, cervical cancer could be eliminated.

I say 'eliminate' rather than 'eradicate' because, in medical parlance, 'elimination' means reducing to a low level, whereas 'eradication' means zero cases, as with smallpox. After researching, I became excited. I realised that vaccination plus screening could eliminate cervical cancer within twenty to thirty years. In a generation!

I punched the air with elation. Vague ambition had coalesced into a more specific purpose: *raising awareness that we can eliminate cervical cancer within a generation.*

It resonated. My daughter Emily narrated a two-minute video I posted on my new website. Ultimately it was viewed over 600,000 times.[1] I gave myself three goals. First, policy: I hoped that CRUK would lobby the government to commit to eliminating cervical cancer by a set date. I knew that Jo's Cervical Cancer Trust was advocating this approach, and that Australia was considering it. Second, I would air the message via local radio, TV, newspapers, and online. Third, I would canvass funds so CRUK could support researchers studying screening.

I flew to England and met Jo in a roadside café near Cambridge on a slate-grey November day in 2017. Jo, a smiling, friendly woman in her thirties with two teenage daughters, was bubbly, cheerful, and organised. Her younger daughter was about to be vaccinated against HPV at school, Jo mentioned. Jo overlaid her practicality with a cheery manner, which softened her scepticism about whether I was serious.

I asked Jo to allocate the funds I would raise for studying cervical cancer screening. No problem, she answered, saying how CRUK is the world's largest cancer research organisation, with thousands of volunteers and high street outlets across the country, supporting hundreds of scientists. Within days Jo had identified a CRUK-supported researcher at University College, London, coincidentally also named Jo – Professor Jo Waller. Was everyone in the cervical cancer world called Jo?

I went on to learn how Professor Waller was examining why nearly thirty per cent of women missed their screening appointments. Did they find the procedure awkward? Or were they too busy? Screening works: since being introduced in the 1980s, UK cervical cancer rates have more than halved. The

---

[1] Find the video at **www.3500toendit.com** or search for "we can eradicate cervical cancer" in YouTube.

researchers were reaching beyond diagnosis to pilot text reminders with pop-up calendars for appointments. I loved this idea. Melitta's periodic cervical check-up had been delayed by a few months because of the normal unforeseen happenings of life: first the doctor had been sick, and then we had been on holiday. That delay of a few months had proven fatal.

CHAPTER 4

PREPARING

Luck is where opportunity meets preparation. — Lucius Annaeus Seneca.

Washington D.C., early 2018

In January 2018, two months after meeting Jo, my phone rang. Outside my Washington office snow was falling and everyone was heading home early. A soft eerie silence was descending on the city.

"Hi, Laurence. We're worried about you."

Uh-oh. I had never heard Jo perturbed before. I suspected that she was unimpressed with the detail of my preparations. I knew I fell into the category of people who do not like arriving early at airports – in contrast to Melitta, who was so insistent on being on time that we once turned up for a 9am flight from Washington's Dulles airport before dawn, when the doors to the terminal were still firmly closed. I teased her for months, until I missed a flight! Beyond putting in place the partnership with CRUK and Professor Waller, my preparations had so far consisted of buying socks and blister plasters. I was in full procrastination mode. But Jo's question was more far-reaching.

"A year is a long time, and the English coast is thousands of miles. And Wales, you know what the weather is like there. 'Specially in winter. So...why not spend a week walking Hadrian's Wall? There's a good path, great countryside, and your friends could join. And it only takes six days."

I guess Jo's higher-ups had asked her to confirm that the crazy guy would do as he said. The CRUK playbook did not include eccentric walkers.

"I can't, Jo," I answered. "I've told them at work I'm going for a year. They're delighted to see the back of me. Too late to say I'll only be gone for a week."

I had shared the plan with family and friends, several of whom promised to join. I couldn't backpedal now. Deeper down, the thrill of the challenge and uncertainty lurked. A change from the humdrum. Unknown unknowns.

"OK," replied Jo. "But we haven't had someone try this before," she continued.

"We're signing an agreement, aren't we?" I replied. "Let's make it clear that I'll walk around all of England and Wales, without skipping any parts, for a year. I must show HR I won't sit on a Caribbean beach."

Jo's voice softened. "Ok, we're on – or rather, you're on – so long as I can check in on you every week. Maybe even join you on a few sections."

Things were fitting into place: a year off work, a charity partner, and a purpose.

A few months later, and two weeks before I began, I had an encounter with a virtual stranger. In retrospect, I should have paid more attention to our conversation. I had met the man only once or twice at work and was surprised when he suggested a coffee "to discuss something important." We sat near the cafeteria, surrounded by the hubbub of trays being cleared away. After some chit-chat, he caught me unawares.

"How do you expect to change as a result of your walk?"

I stumbled out a weak joke about how I hoped to lose weight.

He shook his head and stated matter-of-factly, "You'll change; I guarantee it. Not in ways you can predict."

I thought further and said I hoped the year would help me manage my grief. The man nodded, signalling that there would be more. He stroked his chin stubble, looking squarely at me.

"Depends on whom you meet. They'll change you. In ways you could never imagine," he added mysteriously.

I asked him how he could be so sure, and he told me how he had cycled across the US twenty years earlier to raise funds for charity. Life-changing, he affirmed. When I asked him what he had learned, he told me stories—meandering tales garnished with more meaning than first apparent, almost parables. But my mind rambled away on its own paths, along wayward trails of organising the next few days. I listened only enough to nod at the right times.

In hindsight, another life-altering moment had slid past. Although not nearly as romantic as meeting a woman in a bright yellow dress.

Despite not listening properly, my subconscious began noodling away. Inspired by the heart and organised by the mind, the journey blossomed into a quest to salve my soul. The insights would indeed come, just as the man said. Still, I knew nothing of this at the time. The cafeteria emptied, the noise dying away, noticeable more by its absence than its presence, like the dawn chorus. We bade each other goodbye.

A blithe balm of pre-journey confidence settled upon me, akin to the warm feeling after a first beer. In reality, I had only assembled a few pieces of a jigsaw puzzle – the easy, straight-edged outside part.

A few days later, excited and nervous, I boarded a British Airways flight out of Dulles airport in Washington and flew into Heathrow, London. It was time.

THE SOUTH

16TH JUNE 2018 – 7TH JULY 2018
279.1 MILES 6,937 FEET OF CLIMB

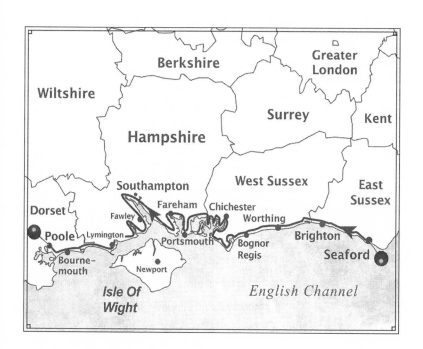

CHAPTER 5

STARTING

"Who has begun has half done. Have the courage to be wise. Begin!"
— Horace.

Day 1, 16th June 2018, Seaford, East Sussex

I chose to begin in Seaford on the south coast, where my mother Barbara had lived since 1979, and finish here a year later. Seaford is an ancient fishing settlement linked to the Cinque ports mentioned in the Magna Carta, a place that never had grandeur to fade. A town where the fresh sea air attracted droves of private schools, which were later replaced by swathes of bungalows.

A few minutes before starting I visited a bench on Seaford's golf course, which we had erected in my father's honour in 2016. My father had been a much-loved man who had captivated my mother's heart on a tennis court in the late 1940s. 'You'd have liked this little escapade,' I thought. My mother was no stranger to attempting unusual feats herself; having climbed Kilimanjaro and flown a plane while living in Tanzania in the 1960s.

Now eighty-eight and wheelchair-bound, my mother came to wave me off at the starting point, the Martello tower on

Seaford's beach. Jo Marriott, and her manager from CRUK, Laura, had also joined me, along with Melitta's younger sister, Tanya, and her husband, Julian. My mother pulled a blanket tight around her shoulders, sheltering from the wind, and bid us farewell.

"Off you go, Laurence, dear. Too windy. Now remind me where you're going, exactly?"

"Well, I hope I'm coming back here," I replied.

"Very good, let's hope the wind has died down by then," she smiled.

Jo told me she wanted me to wave a plastic charity container around while walking. I was eager to avoid that at all costs. I settled on carrying it in my backpack, promising to think about it. Then Jo held up a CRUK flag on a three-foot pole. There was no holding her back.

"What about attaching this to your rucksack so that people can see you coming?"

Was she mad?

Off we strode, our feet slip-sliding on the pebbles, the stiff breeze sculpting a squint in our eyes, our conversation laced with excitement and apprehension.

"Fourteen miles! Never walked that far in my life. Is it hilly?" Jo's voice conveyed mild horror, now planning had morphed into action.

"Couple of minor slopes," I answered without knowing. Jo would remind me of that later with a grimace.

We strolled to Brighton along a track that years ago had simply been the Seaford to Brighton footpath but was now the 'Seahaven Trail'. My first lesson on branding! According to its website, the trail included:

'Stunning views, cliffs, wave-cut chalk platforms, shingle beaches, and a vegetated shingle habitat. The chalk grassland along

the trail is so species-rich that it is considered Europe's equivalent to a tropical rainforest.'

While 'equivalent to a tropical rainforest' was exaggerated, the five of us did hear birds chirping in the long grass, and we enjoyed the flowering shrubs on the cliffs. We gazed down on the foam-flecked waves while exchanging stories, snapping photos and straying nervously close to the cliff edge. The hours passed quickly in the morning, leavened by a mug of steaming coffee in Newhaven. But time, and our legs, slowed as the sun dipped in the sky, the colours softened, and our conversation became more muted.

For a few minutes, in mid-afternoon, I was alone.

I stopped, watching the butterflies dancing over the long grass, undulating in the breeze. Suddenly, behind me, the dry grass rustled. I turned, expecting to see a bird searching for seeds, such as a corn bunting. Nothing there. Strange.

I stepped further into the knee-high grass, wondering.

Without prompting, an image of Melitta flashed into my mind. We had taken an afternoon hike in a rocky valley. That would have been twenty-seven years ago, when we lived in the small, landlocked southern African country of Swaziland. I remember carrying our fifteen-month-old firstborn, Emily, in a backpack, eagerly waving her little arms at the world. Melitta held her camera and sketchbook, veritably hopping from stone to stone, overjoyed with life. She exclaimed with delight at the aloes and proteas growing among the rocks. We had walked barely two hundred yards before she crouched down with her sketchpad. I marvelled at her enthusiasm for the natural world, her ability to memorise impossibly Latin-named plants and to sketch them with a few deft strokes. I settled onto a boulder, lifted Emily onto my lap, and we watched Melitta sketch the aloes, basking in her rapture and the late afternoon highveld sunshine. A lock of Melitta's hair fell over her forehead, interrupting her concentration. She brushed it back and turned to smile at us, warming the chill of the waning light.

The grass rustled again and this time it was Julian.

"So, what do you think – will Chelsea be any better next season?"

We chatted about our teams, Chelsea and Leeds, but meanwhile I allowed myself a wry smile, thinking that if Melitta had been with us, we would have stopped every few yards to photograph the plants and birds.

The last stretch that day to Brighton pier was along the promenade that would serve the next morning as the finish line for thousands of cyclists in the London to Brighton race. We stumbled past dozens of bikes that you could lift with a finger and buy with a month's salary. We snapped a celebratory photo in front of Brighton pier and made a beeline to the nearest pub. One of the seven marvels of my tasting world is the first sip of a beer after physical exertion, especially on a hot day. Unlike many other experiences, where anticipation often transcends the actual, here the sociable, thirst-quenching, that-was-great-but-thank-God-it's-over sensation was sublime.

Jo grimaced good-naturedly, assuring me she would vet the length of any future legs she might join. She had walked the longest distance in her life – and with a not-insignificant amount of climb. Later, Jo told me that her blisters took a week to heal. I admitted I had blisters too, which didn't augur well for the next day, but we were glad the expedition was underway. We agreed on some ground rules that evening as the beer and wine flowed. Jo would call weekly to check on my physical and mental state. I would record each day's leg using an app (Strava), which showed the route, miles walked, hours spent, and height climbed. Each leg would start exactly where the previous day's journey had finished.

When I told Jo I would donate extra to the cause myself

rather than dangle a collections box in front of people, she laughed. Still, I knew she hid an underlying seriousness under her easy-going manner. I couldn't let her down. Jo grinned over her second glass of wine.

I shared my four ideas about how to approach the year. First, I would stroll rather than march, taking the time to chat, relish views, smell the air, think, and divert to cafes or pubs. Second, I would keep my feet on the ground. This meant no ferries or swimming, so when I arrived at a river estuary, I had to hike upstream to the first crossing point, usually a bridge. Often these were several miles upstream, occasionally for unusual reasons. The river Dart, in Devon, for example, housed the country's naval fleet during the reign of Henry VIII. Bends in the river near the estuary hid the ships from those at sea. King Henry was determined to keep this advantage and issued a royal decree that no bridge be built across the river – to ensure that his navy would have free passage. To this day, there is no bridge connecting the two towns on either side of the Dart estuary – Kingswear and Dartmouth. I also found out that a 'ford' on an Ordnance Survey map is a slippery concept. Some were ancient trails for horseback riders because, from a walker's perspective, one's possessions – including my laptop – had to be held aloft as one waded chest-high through the water. Other 'fords' would be suitable for mud wrestling, or dying a grisly death, sucked into the muck as the tide flowed up the estuary. But how to estimate mud depth by casual examination when wading in would have been unwise? I remembered the Catch-22 facing women decried as witches in medieval times in England. Dunked in village ponds, those who sank were innocent, while those who floated were guilty. Best to avoid fords.

Third, I would track the coast as closely as possible, while staying safe and following the Countryside Code – carrying litter home and leaving gates as they were found. This was fine in

Wales, the only country in the world to have a trail for its entire coastline, and in the three-quarters of England with a coast path. But what to do when the signpost pointed through a field occupied by a menacing bull? Or when the track was routed under cliffs with a sign saying: 'Danger: only passable at low tide'?

Finally, I included all islands connected to the mainland by a bridge, such as Anglesey in Wales and the Isle of Sheppey in Kent. Then there were the 'tidal islands', reachable by foot at low tide, but cut off at high tide. The most famous is Lindisfarne, or Holy Island, off England's northeast coast, but there are sixteen tidal islands in England and another thirteen in Wales. Walking to them at low tide created foot-sloshing, heart-racing moments. Stern notices announced that people regularly drowned from misjudging the speed of the incoming tide. These warnings, and sheer fear, inspired me to jog, sometimes through water levels rising to my knees.

Jo listened, head to one side, idly playing with her drink, glancing ruefully at her feet, as I shared my four ideas. The queue at the bar lengthened as the warm summer evening enticed more customers eager to enjoy each other. Jo smiled. She didn't visibly shake her head, but her thoughts weren't hard to guess.

There's a helluva long way to go, fella. Enough of the big ideas. Time to get on with it. And my feet hurt.

We laughed it off, and Jo reminded me that she had only to hobble to her hotel, whereas I would be walking to Worthing the next day. We parted, both relieved to leave behind the noisy chatter of the pub for the gentle swish of the waves on Brighton's pebbly beach.

CHAPTER 6

LISTENING

"Listening is being able to be changed by the other person." — Alan Alda.

Day 2, 17th June 2018, Brighton, East Sussex, 14 miles

The next morning over breakfast my work-friend 'Alan' asked me. "Laurence, why did you buy that bloody enormous camper van if you're intending to stay in bed and breakfasts?"

Alan lived in Brighton and had kindly offered to host me on my first night. I buttered the toast and admitted I wasn't sure. I explained I didn't want to erect a tent in a howling winter gale and shiver in a cold, wet sleeping bag, with stones poking my spine, and how I thought a compact camper van might be the answer.

I shared with Alan how, a few days earlier, two salesmen, whom I mentally labelled 'The Joker' and 'The Silent Postman' had duly serenaded me at the local camper van retailer. The Joker did the talking.

"Amazing, the right van came in this morning, and we've

priced it super cheap fer a quick sale. See that lady leaving? She's just tested it, and she's gonna make an offer, but yer can beat her if yer quick. Now John 'ere, he's a postman, well he were till yesterday, they 'ave to wake up too early, today's his first day with me, 'e'll open the doors fer yer. John, yer gonna love this job, 'specially with customers like this 'ere gentleman. Mr Carter, look at this space, 'cos a good-lookin' fella like you will be meetin' lovely ladies. Sleepin's good fer walkin' 'n walkin's good fer meetin' beautiful wimmen. Stand up, take a shower, make a cuppa, but still small fer parkin'. Park in a pub, so yer don't pay the fees. Have a pint or two, they'll be 'appy. John, take a piccy of Mr. Carter. You're gonna love the price, way cheaper than them VW buses that them agein' 'ippies want, no I can see yer not one, you look like almost normal. Ha, ha, that were a joke, yer not that normal. Them ladies lookin' for a bit of adventure, I can see 'em strolling arm in arm with you along the beach, heh, heh, heh. Now the van were in a minor accident, but she's better than new now, they welded the axle back together. Tell you what, I'll throw in this book about campsites for free. Now, that ol' gal said she'd be back by four, so if yer quick ..."

Bamboozled by the bluster, I signed on the dotted line. A few days later, I returned to retrieve my little camper. As I drove out, the mirror revealed the Joker and the Silent Postman, high-fiving and jumping with glee. They could have had the decency to wait!

Nevertheless, I decided to sample the comforts of bed and breakfasts before resorting to the van. After all, I aimed to share an idea, so wouldn't get far sitting by myself. I booked only Airbnbs with a host, and tried to stay for two nights, using the van for daily logistics. I would park the camper at the start of that day's leg, and after completing the walk, catch a bus or train back to the van and then drive to the next Airbnb. I would plan a week of daily sections ahead and publish them on the website so that friends could identify a meeting point. I also booked a few days of Airbnbs, in a delicate balance between being organized and leaving room for serendipity.

Having a van set me aside from nearly everyone in the virtual club of about fifteen people then circling the UK's coast. Most were 'wild camping'. Furthermore, unlike me, they were all circumnavigating the entire perimeter of Britain, and some overly enthusiastic types added in Ireland and the Shetlands. Like nearly all the others, I would head clockwise, without knowing why. The direction shows up in book titles written by previous walkers. John Merrill, the first person to walk around Britain's entire mainland coast, in 1978, documented his adventures in 'Turn Right at Land's End'. One of the few couples to have completed the feat, Richard and Sally Hunt, chronicled their 10-month, 4,300-mile circuit around Britain in 'The Sea on Our Left'. It seems that walking around the British coast as a couple – unless one of you is a dog – is challenging for the relationship.

Too late, I realized that I had been rambling. Alan was edging backwards towards the door, ready to prepare for our walk that morning, but too polite to cut me off. Suddenly embarrassed, I realized that I had work to do on balancing talking and listening.

"Time to go, day two," I grinned.

Alan nodded, relieved, and a few minutes later we headed out into the early morning Brighton sunshine.

The second day proved to be a harbinger for the year.

Alan and I paced along Brighton's seafront, above the pebble beach. It was still early, so the sun's brightness had not yet morphed into the enervating heat that we knew would arrive by afternoon. The wind of the previous day had been replaced by a gentle breeze, lulling us into an illusory sense of wellbeing. The distant horizon was marked by a newly installed offshore windfarm. Alan would join me for the first few miles to

Shoreham-by-Sea, and then I would continue to Worthing. Although we worked for different institutions on separate continents, we knew each other through work, having collaborated on several projects together. Alan was three or four years younger than me, a tall, determined man, with a disarming smile. I had enjoyed meeting his wife and daughter the previous evening.

For the first hour or so, we caught up on work gossip. And then, in a surprising turn, Alan shared his pain, haltingly, over an unbearable tragedy. Alan's son from his first marriage had struggled with alcoholism in his late twenties. Alan and his second wife tried everything possible to wean the young man off drink and support him. One frosty, late-autumn day, a few months earlier, the police called. His son had died. Alan had spent the following weeks pacing miles along the beach, seeking an outlet for his grief, tormenting himself with what he could have done differently. I listened as he spoke, the pain spilling like an overflowing drain. I was reminded of what Melitta had told me many times when sharing a problem: "I don't want you to suggest anything, Laurence. Just listen."

I realised how levelling and emotionally close the act of walking can be. We shared our experiences in managing waves of grief. I told Alan that sometimes I would be driving, look across at the empty seat, and cry out loud, "Oh Meloo, where are you?". The vacant space would glare silently back at me, and I would pull myself together, blink back to seeing again, and thank God for not crashing in the meantime.

We can't train for grieving, just as we have no notion of the joy of having children until they are upon us. Grief descends, a bleak, heavy curtain of emptiness and despair, waving in the breeze of our memories, and we muddle through, waiting for time to dull the senses. I've heard that men are poorer at managing it than women; they are more likely to die after being widowed. Maybe women are better at managing pain and are more resilient. Or maybe men have weaker social bonds.

Alan and I strolled together in comfortable silence, each of us lost in our memories and glad to share with someone who understood. Our joint reverie ended at a picturesque seaside café near Lancing beach, bustling with a late morning coffee and brunch clientele. There stood Jo, with a welcoming smile, her hair blowing across her face, offering us a cappuccino and threatening to pull out her plastic coin donation container.

I bid adieu to Alan and continued alone to Worthing, struck by his candour. Later that afternoon, I knocked on the door of my Airbnb. 'Tim', a tall and gracious man, wearing his self-confidence lightly, gestured for me to step inside. I gasped. The interior had jumped straight out of *Vogue*. A grand piano partly occupied a living room spacious enough to jog around. Original modern art graced the walls. I knew that Emily would have heard of the artists. Plants adorned the conservatory in the casual-yet-intentional manner of a botanic garden. An orange tree endowed a giant terracotta pot, complemented by a fig tree in the corner. I sat gingerly on a kitchen stool, acutely aware of the state of my clothing. Tim read my mind.

"You're wondering why I'm doing Airbnb," he smiled, putting on the kettle. "Well, I'm not. That's my partner's gig. He'll come later. I'm making my second hundred million. I lost it a couple of years ago, and now I'm on the up again."

I stared at Tim. Was he a Walter Mitty-like figure, living in a fantasy world? The spacious Georgian house on the Worthing seafront suggested otherwise. When I explained my mission, he nodded and told me a story while I leaned against the grey-flecked granite worktop, wondering why the gods had ordained that my first Airbnb should be hosted by a multi-millionaire.

In the early 1990s, he had headed marketing for one of the world's largest manufacturers of refrigerators. Following the

1987 Montreal Protocol on protecting the ozone layer, there was talk of banning CFCs in fridges. One day, the head of government affairs asked Tim for a US$40m budget to pay for lobbyists. Tim asked why.

"To block the proposed ban on CFCs," replied his colleague. "That will kill our fridge business."

"Hmm," replied Tim. "Have you asked the engineers if we could re-tool the production line so they don't use CFCs?"

No one had. A few days later, the answer arrived: yes, it would cost about US$40m and take three months. So instead of spending US$40m on lobbying, the company stopped using CFCs and supported the ban. As one of the first companies to sell CFC-free fridges, it strengthened its market share and increased profits. Tim grinned and offered me another biscuit.

"It's all about asking the right questions," he said.

I loved this vignette. What was the question I should be asking, I wondered? The door opened, and Tim's partner entered, a slight man.

"Paul, this is Laurence, the chap trying to walk around England and Wales."

"Ah, welcome," smiled Paul. "I've bought you a toaster."

Hmm, puzzling. Did I look like I needed a toaster? And then it became clear:

"I'll put it in your room so you can have breakfast there."

Now I understood. The super-sized kitchen and living room were off-limits for the Airbnb guest. Paul the Toast escorted me upstairs to the cavernous bedroom. I couldn't bring myself to ask him why he was hosting people. Financial independence from Tim? Or maybe Tim wanted to talk to Paul's guests; after all, he could have directed me to my room instead of chatting. As I luxuriated in the rain shower, I reflected on Tim's story about CFCs.

How to reframe a problem? *The answer lies in the question.*

I was so pleased with this thought that I repeated it out loud, spraying shower droplets with my breath. But the insight went no further; what was the question? I lay on the bed, refreshed, relishing the ironed sheets, and wrought iron bed frame. I tried some questions out, thinking of the conversation with Alan. Do connections sustain us through loss? What, beyond time, dulls the pain? Does 'doing something' like this walk help? But the questions lapsed, as my energy dimmed.

Later, as I turned off the night lamps and sank deeper into the feather pillows, the toaster positioned by the bedside, I realised that this journey would enable me to plough a furrow into the lessons of life. I dozed off, dreaming of questions and toast.

THE SOUTHWEST

JULY 8, 2018 – OCTOBER 8, 2018
1,065 MILES 145,315 FEET OF CLIMB

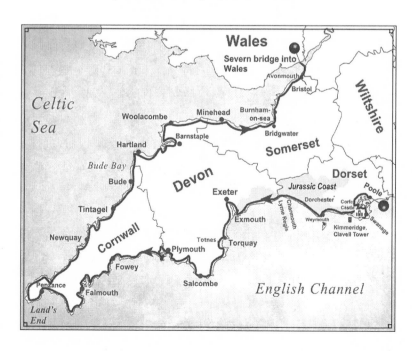

CHAPTER 7

A LESSON ABOUT MYSELF

"We learn from experience that men never learn anything from experience." — George Bernard Shaw.

Day 25, 10th July 2018, Kimmeridge, Dorset, 331 miles

The summer of 2018 grilled the countryside. Luckily England was lasting longer than usual in the World Cup, lightening the national mood, and enabling a temporary respite from the divisions of Brexit. Surprisingly quickly, the miles added up, the blisters disappeared, and my face colour changed from white to red, missing out on the whole tanning stage. In early July I walked along Bournemouth's six miles of beaches, deluged with relaxing people, thinking how much fun it would be to be eight again. I rounded Poole Harbour, and started to walk Dorset's gorgeous, protected coast.

My walking routine was emerging. Drive the van to the end point early in the morning and catch a bus or train back to the start. It felt psychologically safer to be walking towards the van, rather than leaving it at the start and taking a chance with bus timetables late in the day. And before starting, pre-identify a café for tea or lunch. But these practicalities were much easier to learn than absorbing insights about myself. I hadn't realised how the journey would force honest truths upon me.

On 10th July, after twenty-five days, 331 miles and 11,000 feet climbed, my friend Richard joined. An engineer with a twinkle in his eye, and a disarming ability to play both cricket and football at a semi-professional level, we had known each other for thirty years, ever since working on St. Helena. Today we were at Kimmeridge, Dorset, near 'Clavell's Tower'. Reverend John Richards Clavell built the tower in 1830 for contemplation. Vicars in Victorian England enjoyed ample free time, not to mention a generous stipend. This tower reeked of fascinating history beyond meditation: the young Thomas Hardy frequently brought his first love, Eliza Nicholls, to the building for 'hot and heavy' before becoming a novelist. In 2006, in response to the eroding coastline, the tower's owners moved it eighty feet inland. For those wondering how it's done, the answer is to disassemble 16,272 stones, number each one, and re-construct them in order. Perfect for Lego builders!

After passing the site of Thomas Hardy's love life, Richard and I climbed a steep four-hundred-foot hill, sweating on a blistering summer's day. Nearby we found Britain's oldest oil well next to the path, a nodding donkey producing eighty barrels of oil a day. After a mile or two, Richard asked,

"What does Strava say about how far we've walked?"

I used the Strava app to provide a record. Each day, Vanda, my trusty webmaster based in Vancouver, uploaded a scan of each leg from Strava, showing a map with the distance walked, feet climbed, and time elapsed. This proved that each leg began where the previous day's segment finished and that I walked every yard of coastline.

I looked at the phone. "Oh shit, I forgot to turn it on!"

Richard laughed and laughed. "We'll just have to do it

again. Otherwise, some nit-picking git will say that you didn't walk around England and Wales."

He was right, of course. After finishing, we drove back to the start and trudged the first part again. The tower and nodding oil donkey weren't nearly as fascinating, and the hill had grown a few extra feet, but we forgot it all when we settled down with a warm pint in a rowdy pub to watch the World Cup.

"You need a simple checklist," said Richard, between sips of bitter and shouts of encouragement at the TV.

Bloody engineers, why are they always right? I carried a few essential items: Ordnance Survey 1:25,000 map, mobile phone, battery charger, sunscreen, cap, bottle of water, plasters for blisters, a bite to eat, and rain gear. I stored everything else in the camper van. Plus there were a few other steps to remember each time I started, including turning on Strava. I told Richard about the previous day when my sister-in-law, Sasha, had joined.

Sasha had been two years older than Melitta and Tanya three years younger. As an older brother of two, I had never thought about middle-child syndrome before meeting Melitta, but she educated me. How the oldest is the pathbreaker and the youngest needs to be coddled, while the middle one is, well, just there. Melitta regularly reminded me that our son Nic needed special attention. After a hot nineteen-mile tramp, Sasha and I returned to the car park near Corfe Castle, exhausted, ready to slump into the camper van. Except that it wasn't there. Two car parks half a mile apart, and I'd picked the wrong one. I hadn't marked the starting point on the map.

Richard shook his head, laughing. I mentioned that it was worse than that. Earlier in the day Sasha had followed me into a piece of boggy land, singing, "In the jungle, the mighty jungle," and plunged thigh-deep into black, peaty bog. Lucky I'd been there to pull her out, she graciously said. Adding an extra half mile onto nineteen of slogging after having one leg covered in squelchy bog-mud was painful. Sasha's equanimity was remarkable; I would have understood if she had sat down, told me to find the van, and drive to pick her up. During the preceding few hours, she had expounded on yoga philosophy – she ran her own studio – so perhaps she was modelling inner peace. More likely, she thought to herself, *if I let Laurence out of my sight, he'll get lost, and I'll never escape this bloody nightmare.*

Richard grinned. He didn't need to say anything. But I couldn't stop thinking: *Come on, Laurence, you don't need a checklist to put socks on in the morning.* The game was over and England had won. Relieved, dozens of us spilled out of the pub into the relentless Dorset sunshine. A desperate hope hovered over us all, perhaps this was the year England would surprise the country. My phone vibrated; it was Jo from CRUK. Guilt welled through my veins.

"Hi Jo, oh, I'm sorry, I got caught up with supporting England." We both accepted the white lie for what it was. "I'm absolutely fine, blisters have gone, this guy called Richard has joined, claims to be my friend. He can confirm I haven't gone crazy yet."

Richard took the phone.

"Hello Jo, I've heard a lot about you. I ran into a guy on the trail today, he looked delirious. Kept on saying that he had three thousand miles to go. Anyway, he's calmed down now he's had a beer."

Jo laughed and I promised I would call her at our agreed time next week.

I realized that the journey would help me learn about myself as well as honouring Melitta's life. Wasn't that what the man in the cafeteria had said a month earlier? Something about being changed by the people I would meet. And I sensed that the discoveries would go beyond my need for checklists. However, first I needed to hone another skill. One not traditionally associated with men – and I was no exception. Noticing.

CHAPTER 8

NOTICING

"Notice the small things. The rewards are inversely proportional."
— Liz Vassey.

Day 31, 16th July 2018, Charmouth, Dorset, 400 miles

The following week I arrived in Charmouth, thirsty and famished after a long day. A woman in her late forties opened the door to my Airbnb. I had spent the last few minutes calculating. Four hundred miles so far, at an average of 2,100 steps per mile: well on the way to a million steps. And Strava told me that I had climbed nearly 21,000 feet so far: two-thirds of the height of Everest. Meanwhile, my hostess had smile lines around her eyes and an air of rumpled kindness.

"It was you! You did it," she exclaimed.

Startled and wondering what crime I'd committed against this woman I'd never met, I stumbled, "Er, hello Julie, nice to meet you. What have I done? Oh, by the way, here is a bottle for you."

I had fallen into the habit of offering wine to my hosts, as it sometimes led to a convivial evening.

"Oh, great, we'll get to that later," Julie said, taking the bottle. "Now come inside and see," she grinned, and I followed her, bemused.

She pointed to a pile of papers on the kitchen counter.

"That letter from the doctor's office telling me to go for my cervical screening has been sitting there for months. I was too busy to do anything about it, but when I saw from your booking what you're up to, I made my appointment. So, thank you!"

"Oh," I smiled, relieved. "That's why I'm walking."

We chatted about cancer screening, and I told her about my experience. When I turned fifty, Melitta reminded me to go for a colonoscopy. I procrastinated, but she bugged me, so I took the plunge one day, swallowing the required gallons of liquid. I'm ashamed to say that it never crossed my mind to reciprocate and push her to consider her health. Sadly, my ignorance was not unusual.

An hour later, showered, and ravenous for a curry, I asked Julie for a restaurant recommendation. Before I opened my mouth, however, she startled me.

"Did you notice anything about your room?"

A minor panic flitted through my weary body. Melitta would sometimes ask if I had noticed her appearance.

"Your hair looks lovely," I'd say. "You must have had it done."

Occasionally I'd mention this without prompting, on the off chance, which would make Melitta shake her head and mutter about how useless men were. Once, after perhaps fifteen years of marriage, Melitta had bought herself a silk negligee and, to my eternal shame, I had failed to notice, until I heard her weeping quietly to herself. My host stared at me expectantly. I fumbled mentally and started babbling about the view, the soothing echo of the waves, the choice of teas. . . my voice trailed off. She smiled, no doubt also thinking how useless men were, but simply gave me directions to the curry house.

The following morning, as I entered the kitchen, Julie raised an eyebrow. I had no answer, so I raised an eyebrow back. I had scanned my room twice the previous evening without identifying anything unusual. She chortled, shook her head, and joined me at the table, supping from her bowl of granola. She had cooked me a glorious English breakfast of scrambled eggs a la Gordon Ramsay, bacon, tomatoes, and sauteed mushrooms. A sprig of dill sat atop the eggs: my host specialised in little touches.

She saw that I had noticed, and said, "Adds a smidgeon of extra flavour."

Noticing someone noticing, now that was a higher mastery. Sherlock Holmes would have noted the ropes of garlic glinting in the kitchen's morning sunlight, jars of burnt-red dried tomatoes, my host's slight Dorset burr, an azure vase with handpicked sweet peas . . . and drawn his conclusions. I, instead, gazed out of the open window, realising that another scorching summer day had begun. Even the birds were conserving their energy. I made a mental note to carry an extra water bottle. My host spoke. My mind was half-elsewhere; I mused about how much I enjoyed English bacon again, after twenty years in the States. While the irresistible aroma is the ultimate challenge to vegetarians, it was a joy once again to taste the thicker, leaner English cut. I had expected chit-chat about the weather or chock-a-block roads.

"I've something to tell you," Julie said. "I have one son, and he was put on this Earth to save the life of my daughter-in-law."

Another puzzling statement by this enigmatic woman. I nodded in a carry-on-this-sounds-interesting manner.

My host's son and her daughter-in-law had met at school and married young. They had spent years trying to have a baby. Eventually, in her mid-30s, her daughter-in-law had fallen pregnant. Much joy all around! Her new granddaughter transformed my host's life. The daughter-in-law had a scheduled post-natal check-up about twelve months after the baby was born. That included cervical screening. Red alert: they found pre-cancerous cells! After emergency treatment, the doctors confirmed that all was well.

"If she hadn't had that baby, she wouldn't be alive! Every time I see my granddaughter, I think she's twice blessed: her mother gave her life, and she gave her mother life." Julie peered at me to check if I had been listening.

I nodded vigorously, repeating her words while spearing the last sliver of bacon.

"If she hadn't had the baby, she wouldn't have had the check-up, and they wouldn't have caught the cancer early enough," I mumbled.

"Exactly!" My host tried to hide her surprise. She clearly thought I was dim. Maybe it was a man thing, or because I still hadn't found whatever she had hidden in my room.

This is the 'Baader-Meinhof' phenomenon, where something we notice for the first time is suddenly everywhere. It was coined in 1994 by a commenter on the St. Paul Pioneer Press' online discussion board, who heard the name of the German terrorist group twice in 24 hours. The more scientific but less memorable term is 'frequency illusion'. When we spot something new, we unconsciously keep an eye out for it and each sighting is further 'proof' that this is now everywhere. Cervical cancer is not nowadays a common disease in rich countries, thanks to the effectiveness of screening and, more recently, the vaccine. In the UK, for example, around 3,200 women are diagnosed, and about 900 women die each year. Nevertheless, I met a surprising number of people who knew someone who had suffered from this terrible disease. I had the first inkling when I sent out a broadcast email on my last day at work. Among the hundreds of 'good on yer, mate' replies, there were several moving notes about a wife, mother or sister who had died. Now, I was hearing the stories in person, both tragedies and lucky escapes.

Perhaps Julie was simply dredging her mind for conversation topics. Or maybe it was the curious, fleeting intimacy of knowing that we would not see each other again. Either way, I felt that there might be something more potent than pure coincidence at work. I wondered whether Melitta's spirit was keeping a watchful eye.

Fortified by the bacon and the story, I strode up to my room, ready to pack up and head out. Then I saw it! My name was spelled out in Scrabble letters on the bedroom door. I bounded downstairs to tell Julie. She beamed, and we parted, each replete and complete.

The Airbnb experiences were turning out to be richer than I had expected. Everyone had their quirks, their stories, their perspectives. I was enjoying the socialising; it felt right to stay in Airbnbs with a host. Our chats seemed to slide beyond the mundane, especially when fuelled by a drop of wine. I was learning about myself, feeling energised and sensing the benign presence of Melitta. Early days, but I sensed a lightening of my spirits. I set off that morning with a jaunt in my step. My brother-in-law, Julian, was joining for a few days, which would be fun.

CHAPTER 9

YOU'RE JOKING

"Story is a yearning meeting an obstacle." — Robert Olen Butler.

Day 55, 9th August 2018, Plymouth, Devon, 644 miles

"Hmm," muttered Julian, looking at the ten-foot-high set of brambles running the length of the hedge, "that doesn't look too hopeful." We were truly bogged down, in a field not far from Plymouth. The contrast with the past two weeks of walking along Devon's stunning coast was sharper than the bramble thorn in my ankle. After a stream of cloudless days, a persistent foggy rain penetrated every pore, not to mention our boots. After encountering hundreds of fellow hikers along the South West Coast path, we were suddenly alone, taking the path not travelled at all because of my rule about always keeping feet on the ground – thus walking about thirty miles around the perimeter of Plymouth, rather than catching a ferry across the harbour.

Julian and I had known each other for thirty years, ever since we each started dating the two younger Alevropoulos sisters, Melitta and Tanya. We liked running, we enjoyed being dads, we traded mutual disappointment around our respective football teams over pints of ale, and we listened while our wives did more of the talking.

Now we were facing an impenetrable, thousand-year-old, hawthorn hedge – a hedge which had risen above the field it bounded, as its base accumulated the detritus of hundreds of seasons of leaf fall. One could imagine the Celts, followed by the Saxons, and then the Normans, and finally the plain old mongrel English, sitting at the foot of that green, prickly wall, glugging their flagons of mead, spinning yarns, and wondering – like us – how to pass through it. However, the real problem was more the six-foot brambles surrounding the hedge. Truly Peter Rabbit territory. We prowled the edges, searching for a way through. Twenty feet away, invisible through the impenetrable green wall, we heard a horse clopping on a country lane. I grasped a bramble, trying to push it to one side, but instead collected broken thorns in my skin. A reminder of the night before, as my host had sported a translucent green vase of roses and brambles on her kitchen countertop. I had spent the last hour telling Julian the story of this memorable woman in her late thirties. I had asked her why she was hosting strangers like me via Airbnb. Her house seemed too well-appointed for her to need the money.

"Because I'm trying to find someone," she had answered, with a winsome smile.

I wasn't expecting that! Eleven in the evening, and we were into our second glass of wine, sitting on hand-painted stools in her kitchen. By coincidence, she and I had arrived back that evening at her home simultaneously, she after yoga and a wine bar with a friend, and I after fish and chips and a couple of beers with Julian, who was joining me for four days. 'Mindy' had suggested that we open the bottle of wine I had produced on arrival a few hours earlier. As we chatted, I had realised that every gleaming appliance in the kitchen was top of the line; indeed, the whole house was an Ikea-free zone. Careful, coordinated, tasteful, expensive decoration. An understated but deliberate style. A feeling of embarrassment meandered over me, as I wished that I had avoided a wine with 'Tesco' on the label.

"But what about dating sites? Waiting for the right guy to knock on your door is a bit haphazard, isn't it?" I ventured.

Mindy was diplomatic enough not to agree emphatically. Much as I might wish that I was debonair and charming, the reality was that I was scruffy and lopsided, not to mention being twenty years older. In contrast, Mindy was an engaging woman who seemed to have her life together, although her smile hinted at a more profound sadness. With a slim, athletic build, dark curly hair held back with a scrunchie, a friendly manner, and an infectious laugh, Mindy was easy to talk to – especially with the wine.

She finished the glass, nodded for me to split the remainder of the bottle, and said, "You can find out a lot about someone by how they behave in your house. Like, for example, whether they clean the shower."

Yikes! Had I cleaned the shower earlier that afternoon?

Mindy laughed, seeing my confusion. "Oh, you're OK; the shower was spotless."

Hmm, was that true, or was she flattering me?

But Mindy's mind was elsewhere.

"I'll tell you something that you won't believe." Indeed, she did.

A few years earlier, Mindy had decided that she wanted a family. She had a decent job advising the social services department on protecting children from parents who were caught in addictions or were violent. She was pleased because that day she had recommended that grandparents care for two young siblings rather than being fostered, and the judge had agreed.

Then, Mindy continued, she had met The One. An ex-officer with the Grenadier Guards. A man who studied the Bible each day. Although Mindy wasn't religious, she admired his piety. Easy on the eyes, looked after himself. A true gentleman, she said, who called her each day to tell her that he loved her. Admittedly, he had time on his hands, as he was only employed sporadically. Something about a back injury left over from his time in the army. Mindy met his mother, who assured her that he was a most diligent son. After a few months, he moved in, two years later they were engaged, and the date was set. They booked a pre-wedding holiday in Cuba. Mindy arrived home after her last day at work before leaving, grasping flowers she had bought her fiancé, and was surprised to find him sitting on the stairs next to a suitcase.

Mindy hopped off her kitchen stool, reached into the fridge, and found a half-open bottle of white. No 'Tesco' label on that one. She refilled our glasses.

"Good news and bad news," said Mindy's fiancé. "You know I've been trying to get a steady job. Today I received an offer!"

Mindy gave him a hug of delight and the flowers.

"But there's bad news, too," he said, eyes averted. "The job is in Europe, and I have to leave immediately. I've booked a flight tonight."

"What. Are. You. Saying?" Mindy stared at him, not sure whether this was a bad joke.

But he was gone.

Mindy wasn't sure what to do. His phone was switched off. She went to bed, distraught, hoping the next day would bring clarity.

Julian interrupted the tale, pointing at a less brambly patch and suggesting that we assault it with sticks, beating back the thorns. We failed miserably, retreating with scratched hands and diminished egos. I continued, relaying how Mindy's bank had called her.

"Madam, we are charging you unauthorised overdraft fees because yesterday your account went from 27,000 pounds to negative 3,000 pounds."

Mindy called her credit card company and found that hefty charges had also been made there the previous day. She returned to bed, devastated.

After two bedridden days and a changed world, Mindy awoke to find her friends at the door. They hauled her back to a vertical position, dried her eyes, and coaxed her into action. The first stop was the bank. No, the transaction couldn't be reversed. There was no way to prove that her fiancé had forged her signature. The credit card company was more accommodating. And then to the police station.

"Ah, yes, relationship fraud, we get a lot of that," said the sergeant, shaking his head sadly. "How much did he take?"

The sorrowful headshaking continued.

"I'm sure that's a lot of money to you, madam. But, relationship fraud, well, its complex. Lots of he-said, she-said. We have a backlog; it will take us a long time to get to it."

"Er, how long is a long time? Two or three weeks?" asked Mindy.

"Madam, you have no idea how many cases we're investigating. Maybe a year."

"You're joking," exclaimed Mindy. "If a guy burgled my house and stole jewellery, you'd open an investigation. Yet here's this man who stole 30,000 pounds – and by the way, he's staying with his mum in the next village – and you're not doing anything? He's sitting there laughing, planning his next move with my life's savings. Probably booking a holiday to Cuba right now."

Julian and I agreed that visiting the fraudster's house with a few guys from the rugby club might work better than the official route. There was more to Mindy's story, however.

Mindy knew that her lover had broken up with a woman

before meeting her, a landlord of a nearby pub. Mindy decided to warn her in case he tried to return. A day later, they exchanged experiences over a glass of wine. He had lived with his prior girlfriend for two years, stolen 5,000 pounds and then moved back in with his mum. The girlfriend had been too embarrassed to report him to the police.

I suggested to Mindy that she should post something on Facebook to warn everybody about the guy.

Mindy laughed bitterly. "Thought about that, but the libel laws are powerful. And he's sitting on 30k of my money if he wants to employ a lawyer. So instead I'm doing Airbnb – to rebuild my savings and finish my kitchen. And I need to find a decent man because I want a child."

I asked Mindy how she would ever trust a man again. Her grin vanished. "That's what I keep asking myself. How did I get it so wrong? How do I find a good man? Please pour out the rest of the bottle, and we can discuss decency in men."

Mindy spoke animatedly, her fingers playing with the wine glass, raising her eyebrows for emphasis, shaking her curls in frustration. We never solved the problem of how to identify decency. Ask your friends, I suggested. She agreed, saying that they had never liked the fraudster. Mindy and I never met again; by the time I woke up, head throbbing, she had left for work, a vulnerable woman helping vulnerable children.

As Julian and I were chatting, the sky darkened, and misty rain turned into a torrential downpour. I was navigating using a soaked Ordnance Survey map and Google maps on a waterlogged phone. At my instigation, we had climbed over a gate and were tramping down the side of a vast, ploughed field, hoping to connect to a country lane. I remembered from school that an acre was the area that a man could plough in a day, walking behind a horse. This field was the modern equivalent, replacing the horse with a tractor. It was enormous – as though Kansas had paid a visit to Dorset. Our boots slurped up the mud from the furrows as the rain spattered down. As we trudged downhill, our boots gathered huge clumps of red clay.

We reached the hedge with the brambles. I scrutinised the map again. Ah, we should not have climbed the gate; the path ran down the other side of the hedge. I cursed my stupidity. We could hear cars splashing by on the lane a few feet away. What to do? Julian and I gazed, through the rain, back up the endless field, with its 500-foot climb, at our enormous, earthy boots. We simultaneously shook our heads. Fortunately, Julian's support for Leeds United, and mine for Chelsea, were life-training for handling disappointment. We mud-clumped three hundred yards along the length of the field's base, finding only a deer as lost and lonesome as we were. Then back again, hunting for any hint of a gap in the brambles. Julian, to his eternal credit, remained positive throughout. Finally, he saved the situation. He found a thick stick, attacked the brambles with gusto, and astonishingly, spotted a hidden tunnel in the base of the verdant wall, no doubt used by animals. Or maybe the Saxons had made it hundreds of years ago. We scrambled through, wet, muddy, and elated. Twenty-five feet later, we were free of the brambles and back on the road to the van.

Later, we discussed luck. Or was it fate or happenstance? We had persisted with the hedge and, thanks to Julian, been lucky. Meanwhile, Mindy had picked herself up and was persevering, but she was still stuck in the mud and the brambles, searching for a way through. She displayed no self-pity and was experimenting with different approaches. I hoped she would succeed. I also noticed something about myself. For the first time since Melitta had died, three years earlier, I had found myself attracted to a woman. Why? Was it because Mindy had been so open and vulnerable? Or was the walk changing me, per cafeteria-man's prediction? And there were other, related questions. Was it OK to start being attracted to women during a walk to honour Melitta? Or was that just a natural outcome of beginning to recover from grief? My first host on the walk, the millionaire, had taught me the importance of asking the right questions. Now I faced a plethora of them, and the hardest kind: those to oneself, about one's emotions.

These questions remained in my mind as I trekked up and down Cornwall's coast path, relishing the coves and the crags, the company and the solitude, and the early, fresh dawns and drawn-out dusks. I rounded Land's End and started to head north. My emotional education resumed just under a month later, in Newquay, on Cornwall's north coast.

CHAPTER 10

FINDING AND SUSTAINING LOVE

"Perhaps we are in this world to search for love, find it and lose it, again and again. With each love, we are born anew, and with each love that ends, we collect a new wound. I am covered with proud scars." – Isabel Allende.

Day 82, 5th September 2018, Newquay, Cornwall, 976 miles

Approaching the one-thousand-mile mark as I arrived in Newquay, I felt like celebrating and was glad I'd accepted my hosts' invitation to join them for an evening drink, after a surprisingly scorching early September day's walk. As I sat with Caroline and Pete on the patio, drinking wine, Pete showed me the new floor for an extension at the Airbnb.

I was surprised and intrigued as I sat chatting with them. Love wafted through the early evening Cornish air, mixing easily with laughter, the clink of glasses, and carefully distanced cigarette smoke. She, with an accent and mannerisms out of Downton Abbey – upstairs – and he, well, he looked like her builder. In fact, he *was* a builder.

Their connection was unmistakable. And captivating.

Caroline was in her fifties, lean, tall, and good-looking with a hearty laugh and blue, smiley eyes, especially when she fixed them on him. Pete was short and chunky, with a twinkle and an uncanny ability to make her smile, chortle, and then burst into uncontrollable laughter. He told his story with disarming simplicity.

"I worked as a butcher for many years until one day my then-wife announced that she had had enough of rising early. Hmm, I thought, she has tired of me. And so, I left, both the marriage and the trade. I returned to my original work – building."

"Just as well," grinned Caroline. "I didn't need a butcher! There's one of those down on the High Street."

She related her history with a touch of sadness. Her husband had disappeared many moons earlier, and then a few years ago, the children had fledged the nest, and she had found herself rattling around in this multi-roomed house in the Cornish seaside town, whirling down into a depression. A friend had suggested she try online dating, which she had approached with trepidation.

Upon learning his trade over their first coffee, Caroline mentioned her house. What was Pete's advice? It was too large and too infused with memories. Should she downsize and move? But the prospect was daunting, and she had her friends in the town.

"I'd be happy to take a look," said he, in his gentle north Cornish burr, to the lady with the cut-glass accent and posh words.

He looked and pondered. Then he proposed an idea that changed her life. Indeed, both of their lives. Had she heard of Airbnb? He would re-design and re-build the inside of the house to accommodate three Airbnb guests with en-suite bathrooms. She would plan the themes for each room. The idea energised her, and they had started 18 months ago. The tale of the conversion, indeed the whole saga, reminded me of Peter Mayle's *A Year in Provence*. The first guest had arrived that spring, staying in the room inspired by the heather and gorse of the nearby moor. As it transpired, the motif took some explaining to the visitor because she hailed from Indonesia, accompanying her son to boarding school. Once she understood, she insisted on visiting the moor and returned, nodding approvingly – it matched the room.

Caroline and Pete relayed this relationship origin story with gusto, finishing off each other's thoughts and adding embellishments, accompanied by hearty quaffs of Burgundy and much merriment. Their words tumbled into the cool of the evening, a waterfall of anecdotes, eddying around with repetitions and clarifications. It was a joyous narrative of the journey, how the house had returned to life, how they chose the theme for each room, and their plans for a vine for the patio. I marvelled that these two people, who had previously inhabited different worlds, would only have possibly met in one way before online dating – if she had called in a builder. Now, here they were, brought together by unfathomable algorithms, creating a life – not to mention gorgeously crafted Airbnb rooms. They had been lost and now were indubitably found.

Amongst the melee of stories and glasses of wine, I compared this couple's story to that of another host a month earlier in Totnes, Devon. 'Ruth' was a lively, lithe, and yoga-loving woman in her early seventies who impressed me with her irrepressible energy and enthusiasm for life. Laugh lines creased her eyes, and she cracked open the bottle of wine as soon as I arrived. I was astonished by her assertiveness – within two hours of my arrival, she had written to her Member of Parliament, suggesting that he advocate for a campaign around cervical screening. She chuckled, explaining that he knew her well. Indeed, he replied the next day, promising to follow up with the Department of Health. A heart-warming confirmation of local democracy! Ruth told me that she used all her Airbnb proceeds to support her PTSD-affected son and his daughter – her granddaughter. Her son had served in Iraq but had not managed a steady job since leaving the Army. Ruth loved to surprise her granddaughter with an Airbnb-financed treat now and again.

We traded stories, sitting on Ruth's covered porch, surrounded by fragrant plants and musical instruments, as the shadows lengthened on the summer's evening. The wine glasses emptied themselves. We bonded over the remarkable coincidence that she and her previous husband were married by the barman-cum-church minister at the Lilongwe Hotel in Malawi – where Melitta and I had had our first date! However, two years earlier, after twelve years of marriage, Ruth's husband had left, so now she was searching for someone. She related a recent dating escapade, laughing and gesticulating.

"I forgot to tick the box saying within twenty miles, and so this man four hundred miles away in Edinburgh contacted me. When I explained that it wasn't practical, he said he'd never seen anyone so perfect and would I fly up to meet him. He would pay. Well, I said, I'll have to stay in a hotel then. He booked a lovely place, with a spa and all."

Ruth nodded at me and then at the wine bottle. She continued her tale, the hint of a smile playing around her lips, while her twinkling eyes suggested she relished the recounting more than the experience.

"He was a professor who had written thirty-three books about something philosophical. I wasn't sure what we would discuss – I'm not into Plato. Anyway, that evening we met, and, oh Laurence, I didn't know where to look. He had sent a photo which must've been twenty years old when he was fifty pounds lighter. He was, well, let's just say he liked going to restaurants, and I like walking and yoga." Ruth sat back and, shaking her head in amusement, took a sizeable sip from her glass.

"How could this happen?" I asked incredulously. "How can the dating site allow people to put old photos in their profiles?" She laughed at my naiveté.

"Do you think they send someone round to check?" she smiled. "Everyone lies, it's only a matter of how much. The idea is to meet and then wow the other person with your conversation." Ruth snorted, albeit kindly.

She explained that the real problem, though, was not his girth. She could get around that, ha-ha, she grinned. Even his conversation hadn't been too bad. However, like most men, she said, he yearned to be looked after, despite the rhetoric on dating profiles about romantic evenings in front of the fire and winter strolls. That wasn't enough. Ruth had set her heart on *living*, not simply existing. She was searching for someone with an *enthusiasm* – beyond eating!

Leaning back in my chair in the company of Caroline and Pete, the witching hour was nearing on their flower-pot-cluttered patio. Caroline leaned over to Pete and whispered conspiratorially: "You know when I started to like you?"

"Ah, at last, I've been waiting for two years for you to tell me you like me," he smiled.

"When you showed me the drawings for re-designing the rooms. A man with a plan, that's what I thought. I can get behind him."

"Well, my dear, I'd much rather have you in front," he countered. "And anyway, what are a few drawings? You created the rooms."

"Ah," she muttered, slurring a little. "You know what you did. You gave me meaning."

"Us," he replied with a gentle smile.

Then, realising it was all too serious, Pete pulled out some drawings and beckoned to me.

"Laurence, what do you think of the plan to build on top of

this extension we're adding here. You could be useful…although I'm not sure how." With that, they started chortling again.

I went to bed feeling both elated and desperately lonely, as though I had read a captivating book but had no one to share it with. The evening was a reminder of what I had once known. Also, despite the blurring from the wine, I knew that their story hinted at another question I should be asking myself but couldn't figure out. This couple had achieved something beyond mutual attraction and infectious laughter. On the ladder of insight, my foot was in mid-air, searching for the next rung.

CHAPTER 11

REVELATIONS AND SERENDIPITY

"Coincidences link us to the unknown and weave us into it."
— Doug Dillon.

Day 91, 14th September 2018, Morwenstow, Cornwall, 1,096 miles

Mid-September, I crossed from Cornwall into north Devon, near the hamlet of Morwenstow. I lingered in the driftwood hut built on the cliffs by an eccentric nineteenth-century vicar, Robert Hawker, as a refuge to write poems and spot shipwrecks. In addition to rescuing sailors from the rocks below, he invited his nine cats and pig to church services and was the originator of the Harvest Festival celebrated in England today. The days were shortening, the waves lengthening, and the feel of early autumn was in the air. Melitta's spirit felt ever-present.

An email appeared:

Hi Laurence, not sure if you remember me, I used to work at the IFC. My sister died from cervical cancer, and I'd love to come and walk with you for 3 days. Sara.

I vaguely remembered Sara. She worked in Africa, whereas I was in Washington. We met once but didn't know each other. A mutual colleague had given her my contact details. *Of course, Sara, I'd be delighted if you could join,* I replied.

A few days later Sara and I set off from Lynmouth, described by the eighteenth-century painter Gainsborough as 'the most delightful place for a landscape painter this country can boast'. The turquoise transparency of the sea in the coves below hinted at the hedonism of the Greek islands – at least until somebody shouted, "Oy mate, wha' yer doin', can't yer read – tha' gate says 'private'," and we retreated onto the right route. About ten years younger than me, Sara was chatty, funny, and engaging.

Sara told me about her deceased sister, who, like Melitta, had found out too late about her cervical cancer. Timing is life; I had since discovered that five-year survival rates for 'localised' cervical cancer are around 90%. In contrast, that percentage falls to 50% if it has spread to the nearby lymph nodes, and if it has metastasised further, only one in six women will live more than five years. I asked Sara about her job.

"Oh, I'm the modern slavery adviser to The Body Shop," she answered.

"Er, what does that mean?" I asked.

Sara helped the cosmetics retailer to verify that its suppliers were not exploiting their workers. She explained how pernicious modern slavery has become – and how in response, major companies are auditing their supply chains. She told me how vulnerable people are coerced into giving pedicures, picking strawberries or stitching clothes for pennies because their identity documents are withheld. I mentioned reading a news report about some immigrant women imprisoned to work in a garden shed.

I carried *The Times* in my backpack and pulled it out at our next coffee stop, searching for the piece. Scrolling through the pages, failing to find the article, my eye instead caught a feature about which UK university was rated as having the best student experience, including attention from tutors. Surprisingly, the winner was the University of Aberystwyth, in mid-Wales. The writer speculated that because the university was so far away from anywhere, the professors had little to do beyond tending to their students.

Melitta had studied agricultural economics there in the 1980s, and her face always lit up when she spoke of those days. She played for Aberystwyth's women's rugby team, which stood her in good stead when she wanted to shock friends with renditions of dirty songs. She became the fencing champion of mid-Wales. Lived in a cowshed on a remote hillside and emerged proficient in lambing. Savoured the wild wind and spray and a drink on numerous winter nights on the seafront. And in between mastering life, she picked up farming and people skills such that two years later, she managed 300 staff in Malawi's agricultural statistics department.

"Well, I went there and loved it," said Sara.

"That's a coincidence," I exclaimed. "Melitta also went to Aber. When were you there?"

They hadn't overlapped – Melitta was three years ahead of Sara. Sara and I resumed our amble along the clifftop path, glancing down on the tiny coves populated with excited children and relaxed parents. Sara reminisced about her university days, mentioning her roommate's lyrical Welsh name: Manon. That triggered a memory. I asked Sara casually,

"That's funny, did Manon have an older sister called Angharad?"

"Of course," said Sara. "There were four sisters, Angharad was the eldest. A wonderful, warm family."

I nearly fell off the path into one of those turquoise coves! This was astonishing. Melitta and Angharad had met as four-year-olds at Sunday school in Kensington; they had attended the same school in London and then studied at Aberystwyth, close friends throughout. Melitta had moved out of her mother's flat at fourteen to live with an old family friend but was also embraced by Angharad and her large, boisterous, kind Welsh family. After university, the girls went to work in separate countries: Melitta to Malawi and Angharad to Spain. When Melitta and I married in 1989, Angharad was sadly unable to attend the wedding, so I hadn't met her. I never met any of the family, although Melitta talked about them often, with great fondness; we had been on different continents. Now, here on a rocky path in Cornwall, was the closest friend of the younger sister of Melitta's soul mate from her young days. Neither Sara nor I could believe it.

What were the chances, I wondered? That out of the eight billion people on the planet, someone would join me who had a deep connection with the family that played an integral part in Melitta's early life? But startling as this encounter was, what happened next made a huge difference to the year's walk.

Sara and I were on our second day. I told her about a meeting I had attended a few weeks earlier in Exeter, hosted by Cancer Research UK for its volunteers. Jo had encouraged me to attend. After my early failings on keeping in touch regularly, I had resolved to do whatever Jo recommended. About fifty of us were grouped in a charmless hotel conference room, listening to the southwest coordinator for CRUK describing how a guy and his mates re-created *The Italian Job*, driving their Minis from London to Turin to raise £4,000.

At the break, I bumped into a man spending a year kayaking the canals of England. Tall, hangdog, and shaggy, and looking as lost as I felt, I figured that we might have faced some similar challenges. I asked him whether the canals were joined up.

"Nae," said he.

"Oh, are you kayaking canals in Scotland too?" I asked, hearing his accent.

"Nae." A man of few words. In fact, one word.

"Ah, what do you do when you reach the end of a canal?" I was struggling to make conversation.

"Whaddya think, laddie?"

"Er, take it out, put it onto a car, and drive to the next canal?" I ventured.

"Aye."

I asked him who knew about his challenge; he said his girlfriend. I wondered whether their conversations were as terse. Giving up on the socializing, I sat down with a mug of tea and thought about what I'd heard. I realised that it not only mattered *what* one was doing but also *who knew* about it. Solitude might be fine for soul-seeking, but if one was trying to influence others, why be the tree falling silently in the forest, or kayaking alone in the moonlight?

Sara laughed and noted that most of these people who were undertaking a challenge to raise funds seemed to be guys. I told her about a couple I met at the CRUK event. In their late sixties, the man and woman co-chaired a village fundraising group, which had celebrated its fiftieth anniversary. Fifty years of coffee mornings, quiz nights, garden competitions for the longest cucumber, art shows, book sales, and sponsored walks, raising £10-15,000 annually, year in year out. The baton passed down the generations. Over £300,000 raised over the years. But their tale wasn't featured; instead, it was the guys who had driven their Minis to Italy. Glamour trumps quiet persistence in the story department.

I said to Sara that I only had about nine months remaining of my one-year effort, and that I needed to raise the profile of my stroll. My fund-raising was fine – many generous individuals had already chipped in £30k of donations – but I cared more about awareness. After three months, I hadn't broken into the media. I shared with Sara that a man called Ross Edgley began swimming around Great Britain in June 2018, the same month I started. He was in the papers (as well as the sea!) every day, with news about his astonishing feat, and lurid tales about the partial disintegration of his tongue. Occasionally I would scan the sea horizon, half-expecting to see Ross overtaking me. While I was lucky to sleep in a bed every night, and still have my tongue, how could I create news about a guy simply walking the coast?

Sara listened patiently, as we climbed and descended along the trail.

"Stop muttering and mumbling, Laurence, and *do* something. Get help. Focus on walking and find someone to do outreach. Let's sit down at the next café and write out a job description."

An hour later, over a mug of builders' tea and a squishy jam doughnut, bolstered by a view over the gleaming morning sea, Sara and I cobbled a few words together on a napkin:

Man walking for a year needs help with contacting social media, local papers, and radio stations. Familiarity with different social media platforms essential. Ability to write a good story critical. All work remote. Several hours a week.

A week later, Jackie, a friend of a friend of Sara's, contacted me. She started work immediately. Within a week, a local journalist was publishing the story. He said he was glad to find me because 'nothing had happened' that week. A few days later, I was interviewed by a local radio station – they slotted me during the afternoon 'drive-time' schedule. Irrespective of whether anyone was reading the local paper or listening to the radio, my boots lightened, and I honed my story. How my wife had reminded me about my check-up, but I hadn't managed the same for her. How I'd stayed with a surprising number of people with cervical cancer stories. How many boots I had worn through. How the kindness of my hosts had touched me.

This was the first of dozens of local media encounters – and the start of my education in appreciating local radio and newspapers. Later, Jackie would secure TV interviews and a feature on the BBC. She and I would only meet in person nine months later, on the last day of the walk. However, my outreach and profile immediately moved onto a higher plane.

If this were a Thomas Hardy novel, fate would have decreed that Sara and I would have spent two days without making the connection to Melitta. I would not have thought about awareness-raising if we had met earlier in the year. It took a hundred days of walking – and a conversation with a laconic kayaker – for the unknown to morph into a problem, crystallised into a solution by Sara. Hindsight's voice was clear: this was all obvious. Alas, hindsight always arrives on the scene late.

I don't believe in angels, although they look fine on Christmas trees, but Sara came close.

CHAPTER 12

BRANDING

"Marketing is no longer just about the stuff you make…it's about the story you tell." – Seth Godin.

Day 105, 28th September 2018, Minehead, Somerset, 1,214 miles

As I traipsed north for the remainder of September, through Devon and into Somerset, the land flattened out. I was relieved to have a break from climbing and descending the steep wood-lined steps of the stony path. By this time Strava had recorded over 145,000 feet of climb in the three and a half months since I had started in June: equivalent to climbing Mt. Everest nearly five times. I remembered that Bill Bryson's book about walking the Appalachian Trail mentioned how the participants typically lost about ten pounds of weight within a few weeks of starting; I had noticed the same, despite a diet rich in scones, crumpets, and beer.

I was busy with interviews. Jackie, my publicist – that sounded professional! – generated leads with local radio, women's magazines, and regional newspapers. Gently, she signalled that I needed better personal branding. Story of my life, I told her. How? Jackie asked me what examples of great branding I had witnessed on the walk. My destination on 28th September provided a good example: Minehead, Somerset.

I mentioned to Jackie that Minehead was the official end point of the 630-mile South West Coast Path, which starts at Poole Harbour in Dorset, winds through Devon and Cornwall, around Land's End, before ending in Somerset. This trail, boasting sublime views, over 114,000 feet of climb, and a place in the annals of the world's great walks, is testimony to the power of citizen activism. It is fitting that the path's symbol is an acorn. Several hundred years ago, the coastal trails in the southwest originated as routes for coastguards to patrol between lighthouses as they sought to deter smugglers. In the late eighteenth century, over half the spirits drunk in the country evaded duty, and so in 1822, the government formed the coastguard to increase revenue – and of course, the cost of a wee tipple! Contrary to folklore, the coastguard was so successful that their paths had fallen into disuse by the early twentieth century.

I learned that in 1972 a Philip Carter (no relation) took a walking holiday on the north Devon coast but found the trails had been swallowed up by brambles or ploughed over. He was blocked when he tried to obtain plans for paths from the Government's Countryside Commission. Eventually, in January 1973, he and some friends held a public meeting in Newton Abbot to set up the South West Coast Path Association. Later that year, over a hundred walkers participated in opening a trail in Cornwall. And over the next five years, the local authorities in Devon, Dorset, and Somerset connected sections, so that by 1978 the whole path was born. Later, this inspired the Wales coast path, which was opened in 2012, and then the all-England coast path, originally scheduled to open in 2020, but delayed by the pandemic.

Jackie listened to me rambling on and brought me back to practicalities. She reminded me that I wasn't starting from scratch. My daughter Emily had designed a T-shirt with a white logo on a teal background. My sister-in-law Sasha had painted the camper van in the same teal colours and included the website address. I was posting weekly blogs. Local journalists were interviewing me. Still, it wasn't enough. Diplomatically, Jackie hinted that I needed to ramp up my quirkiness rating. Walking the coast was worthy but not gripping.

"You need to be weird or funny, Laurence," Jackie explained.

Hmm, I struggled. I had been called many things, but weird or funny was not among them. This doesn't feel easy to figure out, I thought. Then I met 'Jean,' another host.

Jean ran a kitchen in a pub located on a remote beach. In the morning she drove me fifteen miles to drop me off at my starting point, and in the evening she put my soaking shorts in the dryer. As the dryer spun, she regaled me with a tale. On a typical summer weekend day, the pub might host thirty people for lunch – all of whom had to trek a quarter of a mile along the beach to reach the building. Suddenly, over one summer, the numbers trebled. Jean had to re-organise the kitchen and change the menu. Apparently, an online magazine had featured the pub as the third-best beach hostelry in the world! Now everyone wanted to visit. Jean laughed as she told me about the phone call the owner had made to the magazine:

"Hi, I'm calling to thank you for featuring us. You've really increased our business."

"That's great. Why do the patrons like your pub so much?"

"Well, what did your scouts say after they visited us?" asked the publican.

"Scouts? Oh, we didn't send anyone to your pub. It's too far away. Looks difficult to get to, all that walking along the beach. But the Trip Advisor reviews were positive, so we put you in the ratings."

When I relayed the story to Jackie that evening, to my surprise she focused on the dryer rather than the pub.

"Why are you wearing shorts, Laurence, now that it's getting colder? And in the rain."

I liked the air around my legs, I told her. I didn't want to hike in wet jeans and couldn't face the hassle of putting on waterproofs. I had bought gaiters to stop water dribbling into my shoes but thought they looked ridiculous and was too embarrassed to wear them. Jackie asked if I expected to carry on wearing shorts through the winter, and I confirmed that I would. After muttering "Crazy" under her breath, she said:

"Perfect, we'll brand you as 'Man in Shorts'."

As the autumn drew on, and the rain stepped up, every interview turned to my taste in clothing. The shorts were nothing special – typical khaki-coloured, longish shorts with multiple pockets, which were handy for my phone, recharging battery, connection cables, and peanuts. Jackie had taught me that raising awareness without branding was like cooking a meal without inviting anyone to dinner. I was learning how to tell a story. A story about honouring Melitta but now also about how I was feeling and what might come next. I didn't yet have answers to those questions, although I knew that I was beginning to look forward more than I had for the past three years.

Meanwhile, October had blown in, sweeping away the whimsy of summer. After 1,300 miles I was about to broach Wales and winter. It was time for delving and some exploration of the soul as I traipsed along the water-logged coastal path. And I still needed to figure out quite why that evening with the couple in Newquay had felt so illuminating.

CHAPTER 13

FRUSTRATIONS

"You've got to be very careful if you don't know where you are going, because you might not get there." – Yogi Berra.

Day 115, 8th October 2018, Avonmouth, Somerset, 1,344 miles

'Twas the night before Wales. The next day I would cross the Severn bridge and start the 870-mile Wales Coast path – the only coastal path in the world to cover every foot of a country's coastline. A drizzly, cold November evening had settled upon the port town – Avonmouth – where I was spending the night, after a day of urban walking, past anonymous warehouses, gaunt cranes, and empty docks. Ah, I was so ready for a boiling mug of tea, accompanied by a crumpet with lashings of butter... I started to salivate until the water dripping off my nose reminded me that I was still outside. I had booked via Airbnb the day before, pleased to see that I was 'immediately accepted' – and that I would stay with a 'Superhost'. Airbnb had my money; my stay was guaranteed, and my host would be marvellous! After finishing the walk, I drove the van in slowly, searching for the house and a parking spot.

'Mean streets' doesn't fully capture the nature of the neighbourhood. The locality carried a vaguely threatening air. Half of the streetlights weren't working. Sludgy litter blocked the drains. Several of the two-up-two-down houses had boarded-up windows. Had there been trees, their roots would have upended the paving stones – but there was no greenery in sight, apart from a brave weed or two fighting through the trash. Suffice to say that after parking the camper van, I glanced back twice in the three minutes it took to stroll to the Airbnb to check if it was still there. Unyielding darkness and silence emanated from the terraced house, dissipating my dreams of a warm fire and hot sustenance. I double-checked that I had the address correct and knocked. The drawn curtains mocked me.

"Hello, anyone home?" I shouted, with increasing irritation, water streaming down my face.

All was balefully silent. There were no friendly neighbours to ask. I called the Airbnb helpline. The lady in the Philippines was most helpful. Could she find me another place nearby for that evening, she wondered? I gazed around doubtfully. Ten minutes later, she called back and brightly gave me a name and number for a house nearby. I phoned, hopeful but sceptical. To my delight 'Sue' said I could come to stay at 8.30pm.

Result! I decided to celebrate with half a pint at a nearby pub. I strolled over, a spring in my damp step. The sign on the entrance was not reassuring:

'*Anyone caught fighting or taking drugs will be temporarily banned.*'

Temporarily? I wondered why – presumably, the clientele had their days when they strayed, fought, or took drugs, but in the end, I guess the pub's owners believed in redemption. Or needed the business. I walked in. This was a dockers' pub. The not-so-background music was heavy metal, the only women in the room were behind the bar, and the drinking was deliberate. A light dusting of wet sawdust covered the wooden floor, and most of the twenty-odd patrons were heavily tattooed, muscular, and wiry. Not to mention wary of strangers. I sensed a slight easing of the conversation as they sized me up. Admittedly, I did appear strange, wearing shorts on a cold, wet October evening.

"What can I do you for, boyo?" asked the bartender, with a smile, in a lovely, lilting Welsh accent. Ah, I couldn't wait to be in Wales! I thought for a moment how I would answer her. This was not a pub where a guy could ask for a mere half a pint!

"Pint of bitter, please. What've you got? Oh, yes, Brains would be perfect."

I had heard of this Cardiff brewery and their bitter, known locally as 'Skull Attack'. A man perched at the bar nodded at me curtly. Three drained glasses sat next to his latest pint.

"That'll warm you up, son. Bit chilly to be wearing those, isn't it? Where are you heading?"

I was never sure how to answer. Saying I was walking around the coast felt like too much information. Like asking someone how they are, and they describe their health for ten minutes. I kept it short, telling him I would cross the Severn bridge and head into Chepstow the next day.

Shaking his head gently, he muttered: "Rather you than me. Why yer doin' that, in this weather?"

I took the plunge and explained that I was walking around the coast. I asked him whether he knew the coast path nearby. Immediately two things happened – as they did, in pub after pub, each time I had this conversation.

First, the man's face softened from its natural 'life-is-grim' resting state to a wry grimace, as he muttered: "Good on yer. A mate of mine…his wife, she got that cancer, and she's gone now, he's left with two kids, doesn't know what to do, poor git."

It always surprised me how many people knew someone who had had cervical cancer. And how quickly it became a topic of shared stories. Then, the second part: the man called over a couple of his friends.

"Hey John, this fella's walking around the country. Doesn't know the path near here. Wants to stay close to the sea. Isn't the trail closed right now? Can you walk along the beach?"

The guys warmed up. No, the trail wasn't closed, but it's overgrown… better to use the beach…but wait, you can only do that at low tide…what times are the tides tomorrow…oh, noon high tide, that sounds risky…no, you can walk along the top when the tide's in, my girlfriend and I did that only last week…whoa lads, listen to this, Alec is getting serious, walking with Jill on the seashore…you should try it sometime, get some fresh air…whaddya mean, I walk down here to the pub three times a week, plenty of exercise…what Jill sees in you I've no idea… I know, it's his tattoo that says '*Alec and Carrie*'…what does Jill think about that, eh …hey lads, enough, we need to tell this fella where to go…well first he needs to buy himself some jeans…

Eventually, drawing on the collective knowledge of the group, I was advised on the next stage of the walk. This happened dozens of times during the year, and it was always helpful and energising. They wished me well, and, fortified by the warmth of the Brains and the discussion, I headed out into the drizzle. Thankfully the camper van was in the same place, and five minutes later I knocked on the door of my saviour.

Paradise!

Sue's house was cosy and embracing. A real fire graced the living room. Plants, books, and paintings were scattered around. She had laid a place for me and lit two candles. Would I like a hot drink? Could she put those crumpets in the toaster for me? A friendly, chatty, bustling woman about the same age as me.

After a shower, I relaxed at the table, watching the shadows from the candles dance on my butter-laden crumpets. Relaxation infused my body in the way our eyes take in autumnal colours – gently, with wonderous, calm pleasure. Just as well the original host was away, I thought. Through my fog of tranquillity, I heard Sue clearing her throat.

"Do you mind if I sit with you?"

Of course not, said I. I was expecting the usual inquiries about how I managed with blisters, and how many boots I had worn out. But no. Too late, I realised that I was the lobster in the pot, and the water was warming.

"So sorry to hear about your wife. What drugs was she treated with?" asked Sue.

I said that she had been prescribed a cocktail of different types of chemo, plus radiation. The radiation was worse, as it had damaged other organs nearby.

"What about turmeric? And ginger?" Sue pressed.

She asked about other herbs, many of which I had never encountered. I explained that, yes, Melitta had combined medicinal herbs with other dietary changes and taken prescribed drugs. I also said that what Melitta valued most during the three years between diagnosis and death was emotional support, from her family, friends, and a fantastic non-profit, Hope Connections, which offered yoga, art classes, and meditation for cancer sufferers and their caregivers.

Sue wasn't listening. There was no holding her back. Had I heard of doctor so and so, from the States? I should have lied and said yes. Sue explained that he had proven that cancer sufferers could be treated purely with herbal remedies and that modern medicine was killing its patients. As for the HPV vaccine. . .well, this doctor said a plant-derived compound worked better. I listened politely for a while, slowly realising that wasn't a conversation. The lecture was still in full swing an hour later, but the candles and I were struggling. My tolerance melted with the wax. I backed out of the room, protesting that I had to make an early start the next day. Sue threw out one last vestige of herbal advice as I trudged up the stairs.

A shot glass containing a dark green, foul-smelling liquid stood on the bedside table, accompanied by a note saying this would give me energy. I poured it into the basin, my spirits low, knowing I needed to learn to deal with obsessive people. But, of course, I was obsessive too. We all have our enthusiasms, compulsions, and delusions. Maybe it's how we share those with others? Rather than proselytising, I liked to think that I was in the 'live and let live' camp. But I also knew that change doesn't happen without advocacy. My head spinning with irritation at myself, I was almost asleep when a text arrived:

'Hello, you must be my Airbnb guest tonight. Sorry if I wasn't there. I'm in Italy for the week, and the connection is bad. My friend has a key and can let you in. Airbnb wants to cancel the booking, but we can sort it out.'

'Sorry if I wasn't there?' There was no IF about it, you idiot. How did you become a Superhost? Ah, if only you had been home, I wouldn't have faced this barrage of tasteless advocacy. I switched off the phone with a sigh and tried to fall asleep, but instead thinking about Melitta, wondering how she would have handled a host like Sue, who insisted on ramming her views down my all-too-open throat?

Lying there, an image of Melitta, eight months pregnant with Georgie and opening the door to a guest, came to me. A man in his seventies had come to stay with us, ostensibly to see my collection of old St Helena books. Melitta's view was that he simply wanted a free night. His name was Quentin Keynes and he was the nephew of the economist John Maynard Keynes and the great-grandson of Charles Darwin, and he had made his life as an explorer and raconteur – and as their relative. He had visited St Helena in 1950 and wrote the first National Geographic article about the island.

When I arrived home from work, I saw that things were off to a bad start. Quentin had told Melitta that his bags were in the car, expecting her to carry them in. Melitta had waddled out to fetch his leather bag, and had made dinner, but she was drawing the line there. The situation worsened when I set a fire in the living room for the first time that winter, discovering too late that the chimney was blocked. Smoke filled the room, forcing us to throw all the windows open to the freezing air. Later, over dinner, when Quentin would normally have been in full raconteur mode, Melitta instead firmly steered the conversation to other topics. Each time Quentin started to speak, she intervened and then finally announced that he must be tired after his travels, how he needed an early start in the morning and that it was bedtime.

Although I left Sue's house early the following day to avoid a breakfast tirade, she sent me emails explaining what to do with nettles and liverwort. As I crossed the Severn Bridge into Wales, the breezy, sunny morning and open aspect restored my spirits. As I strolled, some weathered pieces of card attached to the railings caught my eye. *Wait! Call this number before jumping. Your life has meaning.* I leant over the railings, wondering just how desperate –and courageous – one had to be to throw oneself onto the hard, glistening estuary below. As I stood there musing, knees a little shaky, I realised, belatedly, that "meaning" was the key to my experience with Sue, and the Cornish couple. Sue derived meaning for herself from advocating herbal remedies to all and sundry, even if they didn't always respond. And Caroline and Pete and found meaning superficially in renovating her house for Airbnb guests, but more profoundly from each other. I tried to turn this train of thought onto myself but couldn't quite sort it out. Honouring Melitta through advocating for ending cervical cancer was certainly meaningful, and that was being reinforced by the people I was meeting along the way. I stepped off the bridge, glad to have arrived in Wales.

WALES

OCTOBER 9, 2018 – JANUARY 9, 2019
941 MILES, 78,597 FEET OF CLIMB

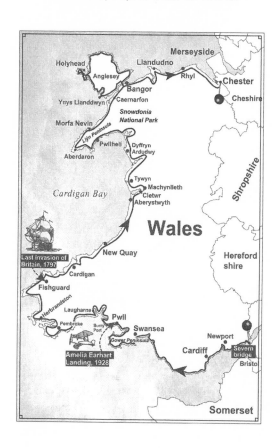

CHAPTER 14

TESTING WATERS

"It is only when we are truly alone, without someone else to lean on, left with our own inner solitude that we can undergo a process of change." – LJ Vanier.

Day 137, 30th October 2018, Pwll, Carmarthen, Wales 1,582 miles

The late October day in South Wales began well enough. After parking the van at the end of the walk and busing back to the start, I decided to photograph every flowering wildflower. I struggled with names after dandelion and honeysuckle. Then, as if the gods were teasing me, I chanced upon a meadow overflowing with late-autumnal blooms. I abandoned the categorising and lay down for a few minutes, eyes closed, inhaling the aroma, imagining how Melitta would have savoured this moment. As a woman who occasionally expressed irritation about how men dominated lists of famous people – "Men celebrating men," she would mutter – she would have also enjoyed a plaque I happened upon an hour later, celebrating Amelia Earhart's crossing of the Atlantic, the first by a woman. After a twenty-hour flight, she landed in the Pwll estuary on

June 18, 1928. Incidentally, the village of Burry Port, two miles away, makes an equal claim because Earhart stepped ashore there.

Earhart's achievement reminded me of one of my favourite books, which Melitta had given me, and I was carrying now. In *West With The Night*, Beryl Markham describes how in 1936, she became the first person to fly solo, non-stop, from Britain to North America. After the book languished in obscurity for many years, a letter from Ernest Hemingway to a friend was discovered in 1982, which led to the book being re-published:

'Did you read Beryl Markham's book, West with the Night? ...She has written so well, and marvellously well, that I was completely ashamed of myself as a writer. I felt that I was simply a carpenter with words, picking up whatever was furnished on the job and nailing them together, and sometimes making an okay pigpen. But this girl, who is to my knowledge very unpleasant and we might even say a high-grade bitch, can write rings around all of us who consider ourselves as writers ... it really is a bloody wonderful book.'

There followed a controversy about whether Beryl Markham wrote the gorgeous, straightforward prose in her book.

She did.

I looked out over the Pwll estuary, imagining one of those old biplanes struggling in, buffeted by the wind, sucking up the last drops of its fuel after flying low over the Atlantic waves for hours, and shook my head at the courage and foolhardiness involved. As if reading my thoughts, the clouds closed in.

The rain returned.

By late afternoon, my mood changed. The full moon hung heavy in the night sky, filtered through the mist and clouds, adding shades of grey to an otherwise black evening. It was only 5 p.m., but it felt like midnight. At least the rain had stopped after an on-off deluge lasting what seemed like a week but was probably only two days. I thanked the Lord that my van was around the corner, with dry towels and heating. A droplet of water trickled down my back, reminding me that a 'waterproof' anorak only goes so far. I hitched up my backpack, treading carefully on the wet leaves, trying to avoid the potholes and puddles on the gravel road following the estuary. The sign said, 'Prone to flooding', but so far, I had been lucky. The night felt silent, eerily so, and I realised the wind had vanished with the rain. However, a still, biting chill was settling across the sodden land, and soon the standing water would turn to ice. My boots crunched the frosting gravel loudly. I fantasised about hot tea as I trudged forwards, tired after a fifteen-mile slog, barely glancing at the water a few yards to my left. I rounded the corner and saw the van where I had parked that morning, at the end of the walk, atop a slight incline, about a hundred yards ahead. Fantastic! There was only one problem: the moon's faint rays were reflecting on the path ahead, which meant water.

To my right, there was an almost-vertical thirty-foot slope covered in brambles. No chance to climb around and above the flood. My boots were soaked through, so a little wading wouldn't hurt. There was the van, so close! I stepped forward gingerly, watching my feet disappear. Oh dear, deeper than expected. But the van was closer now. I estimated that there were a hundred and fifty steps to go. Next, my shins disappeared, and then my knees. The chill of the water penetrated through to the bones of my legs. The smell of the estuary permeated the air, a mix of salt, sludge, and vegetation. I stopped, wondering. Turning back would involve a detour of at least two miles. Versus a hundred steps to safety. I took my laptop out of the rucksack in case the water became deeper. I knew I shouldn't have brought it but leaving it in the van had seemed riskier. Standing knee-deep, I clasped the laptop, wrapped in plastic bags, to my chest, and tentatively moved my feet. By now it was pure guesswork where the track lay. Stray a few feet left, and I would be sucked into the silt of the estuary. The water inched higher, up to my thighs, hips, waist, and then above the belt holding my shorts. Was the tide rising that quickly, or was the track heading down a steep incline? My teeth began chattering, reflecting the chilly water, wintry air, and feeling psychologically low.

Something brushed against my bare legs. I jumped, my curses trailing through the frigid, silent night. The whole 'man-in-shorts' gig felt stupid now. A fish? Underwater flotsam? A water rat? My imagination roiled with images of hungry critters nipping at my tasty shins. Something changed, suddenly, almost as if a switch in my mind had flipped. This could not go on. I strode ahead, done with the six-inch probing steps, holding my laptop high above my head, watching the water rise above my stomach to my ribcage. Even if, God forbid, I had to doggy-paddle. Decisiveness felt good, and the water remained at the same level on my chest. And then, it began to fall, down my ribs, to my belly button, and then to my hips. Within two minutes I reached a slope leading up to the van, the water receded, and I stepped out, dripping, my shins intact, my psyche recovering.

Twenty minutes later it was just a memory, as I warmed myself with a mug of tea in a nearby supermarket café. The attendant was preparing to leave for the day, hinting by offering to mop every square inch under the table and my chair. The clock said ten minutes to closing time. I promised her I would clear up my tray if she wanted to leave; she flashed a quick smile and disappeared. I warmed my hands on the tea pot, relief coursing through my veins as palpably as the tea. I glanced towards the rain-spattered window, through which I could see the harsh glow of a streetlight reflected off the ice. My thoughts drifted back to a painful time, a time when we lived with ice for months, when the children were aged between six and eleven.

We lived in Warsaw, but I flew every Sunday evening to

Moscow for work, leaving Melitta alone in a place where she knew few people, where the sky was grey from October to April, and where the biting wind accelerated across Poland's plains. Melitta looked after Emily, Nic, and Georgie, running them to and from school during the week, until I returned on Friday night. We were both exhausted and often irritable. One winter Sunday, after months of this, Melitta suggested a walk with our dog. We had a few hours left before my departure. The children ran ahead, chasing each other and our dog on the flat, litter-strewn grassland near our house. A giant coal-fired power station belched fumes, as if painting a darker hue over the grey canvas of the sky. Thankfully, the wind was blowing the fumes away from us that day.

"Laurence, we can't continue doing this. This setup is destroying our family." Melitta was clear.

I knew she was right. In Moscow, the next day I told my boss I would leave Warsaw or the organisation within a month. Luckily, a job opened in Washington; sometimes life works out. Melitta filled with life again, and the family recovered with her.

The supermarket café lights had dimmed and the attendant started stacking the chairs upside down on the tables. Time was up for my reminiscences. I placed the teapot on the counter, still half lost in thought. I wondered whether Melitta's spirit had somehow intervened with this wading escapade. At the very least, I sensed fate holding some guardrails for those times when my follies gained the upper hand.

CHAPTER 15

MELITTA'S SPIRIT

"A world in which there are monsters, and ghosts, and things that want to steal your heart is a world in which there are angels, and dreams and a world in which there is hope." – Neil Gaiman.

Day 170, 2nd December 2018, Aberystwyth, Ceredigon, Wales 1,761 miles

I arrived in Aberystwyth a month later, in early December, after walking around the glorious Pembrokeshire peninsula. Although I had never visited Aberystwyth, I carried a picture of it in my mind. Melitta had studied agriculture at the university for four years, loved the town and would regale us with stories of rugby games, stormy nights on the pier, and sheep giving birth. My engineer friend Richard, who had reminded me early in the walk that simple lists might save me from my forgetfulness, had driven for five hours to join me for the weekend – to give his Mazda Miata practice on the Welsh hills, so he said. We stumbled into the town, weary after a gale-laden ten-mile stretch, an afternoon of bending low and holding onto tufts of grass to survive the wind.

Someone had told me there are twenty-five words in Welsh for wind and rain, ranging from a light, misty, damp breeze to horizontal, hurtling sheets of water. I doubt it. That isn't nearly enough. On slow days, I would entertain myself by making up my own examples of Welsh words for the gradations of wind:

No wind: 'dim gwynt'. Once in a blue moon – so rare that you'll remember the occasion for the rest of your life. Like seeing a snow leopard in the wild.

Gentle breeze: 'awel ysgafn'. An unusual occasion to be remembered with a fond smile. Like a first date.

Howling gale: 'galeu calon'. Regular, normal occurrence. Like on Mondays. Not to mention Tuesdays, Wednesdays…

Today had been a 'galeu calon' plus day, such that Richard and I could barely hear each other even when shouting. It was a relief to descend from the exposed cliffs down into Aberystwyth, a genteel-looking town, with a curving promenade of Victorian buildings facing the sea. It was 4 p.m. and dusk was encroaching on the wan afternoon light. We strolled towards the pier, to watch the waves crashing into its spindly iron legs. I could hear Melitta's descriptions in my mind.

Indeed, the last few weeks had been downright spooky. Wales enveloped me, like an octopus spreading its tentacles, in a space bounded by memories, coincidence, imagination, and the supernatural. First, there had been the lunch arranged by Sara, after our walk in Cornwall, where I discovered that she knew Melitta's oldest friend, Angharad. Sara had asked me whether I wanted to contact Angharad and her sister, Manon. Of course! So, in mid-October we had all met for lunch in Cardiff: Angharad, Manon, another sister Rhianon, and their parents, Mr and Mrs Davies, who, in the late 1970s had embraced Melitta as a fourteen-year-old, escaping the stepfather she loathed. Coincidentally, the table was loaded with olives, hummus, fresh tomatoes, feta, and other delicacies which Melitta and I had eaten on trips to Athens to see her Greek father and grandparents. It was a strange feeling. Ostensibly we were sitting in the kitchen of a suburban home in Cardiff, the light from a bright autumn afternoon streaming in. But the melee of table-laying, questions, jokes, stories, and old photographs time-travelled me back forty years to the Davies' house in London which I had never seen, where Melitta had spent days as an extended member of this extraordinary family. Here was Melitta as a girl and young woman. Naughty, feisty, and vulnerable. Teenage Melitta stared out of the black and white photographs, with her mischievous smile, and a firm jaw, unruly curls, and hurt eyes. The tales swamped me, everyone describing and embroidering simultaneously. Occasionally, the raucous chatter would stop for a second or two of silence, and then, as if no one could bear it, everyone would start again.

Of course, they wanted to know about Melitta as a grown woman. I cannot remember what I said. It would have been around Melitta as a mother. Perhaps I told of one evening on St Helena, a month after Emily had been born. My friend Richard had dropped round with a couple of beers and instructions from his wife to behave responsibly. We had all agreed that Melitta deserved an hour off full time motherhood, to have an hour with her girlfriends. Richard and I were on duty to look after sleeping Emily, who lay peacefully in a bassinet in the corner of the room. Melitta drove away, tyres crunching on the gravel, and we settled down with our beers in the small living room of the house perched on St Helena's steep hillside, overlooking the Atlantic ocean. The only sound was the steady breeze from the south easterly trade winds. At which point Baby Emily opened her eyes and took a deep breath. The power of her little lungs was astonishing, as she screamed relentlessly for the next hour, impervious to the efforts of Richard and me to carry her, pat her back, offer her a bottle, or sing songs. We might have even offered her a drop of beer. As soon as the baby heard the car returning, an hour later, she closed her eyes, exhausted, and was fast asleep by the time Melitta walked in, saying "Well done, boys." Then she saw our haggard looks and after a good chortle, she empathized and suggested that next time we could all go out together, bringing Emily with us. I realized then just how easily motherhood had come to Melitta. Angharad and the family nodded; they knew through Melitta's letters how she had evolved from the stressed girl they had taken in, to the assured woman.

Angharad's mother, who worked as one of the first female judges in London in the 1970s, told stories of how there were no toilets for female court officials until she lobbied for them. I am sure that Melitta was influenced by this remarkable woman. From the first moment we met, Melitta would remind me that there was no good reason for men to lord it over women, for right-handers to dominate left-handers, or for man to control the environment. As I drove away in the van after lunch, I could not help but wonder if Melitta's spirit had arranged the rendezvous. On the Pembrokeshire coast in mid-November, she appeared again.

I was staying at a 16th century farmhouse on the northern part of the Pembrokeshire coast, near Fishguard. A place with creaking floorboards, crooked ceilings, unexplained noises, and history oozing from the walls. I slept badly as the night was beset by moaning wind, rain spattering on the thick windows, and strange banging sounds. At last, in the morning I awoke, still half-asleep. Everything had calmed down. The early dawn rays suffused the room with soft light, highlighting the grain on an old wooden cupboard. Rose-decorated curtains clashed with the mustard walls. The wind had decreased to an unsteady whine. I blinked, and closed my eyes, searching for my mind's on-switch, to remind me where I was, still half-lost in my dream.

"Laurence." The voice was quiet, firm.

The dream vanished, despite me not wanting to let it go.

"Laurence." Same voice. I recognised it immediately.

"Yes, Meloo," I replied, instantly awake, surveying the room. "Where are you, my beautiful?"

Nothing. Silence. I listened for a minute, desperate for her return.

Eventually, I concluded that my brain had cruelly teased me.

Now, having arrived in Aberystwyth on a brooding, blustery Sunday afternoon, Richard and I were surprised to see a dozen people leaning on the railings, gazing out to sea. We had seen hardly a soul all day. Then we spotted what they were watching: thousands of starlings swirling up and around the pier in a magnificent murmuration. Eddying and whirling in astonishing synchronicity, the birds dipped down to the white-topped waves, and rose over the pier, lost in the joy of the moment. We stood agape, silent, taking in nature's spectacle until the light faded to a slate-grey dusk.

It felt as if Melitta's spirit was welcoming us to one of her special places. My thoughts wandered to a conversation with Melitta, a few months before she died. I knew something was on her mind; she seemed perturbed.

Lying awake in the bowels of the night, knowing that I was sleepless, she murmured:

"I've something to tell you."

"Mmm?" I replied.

"I want you to find someone after I'm gone. To care for and be happy with."

I wasn't ready for that, either the conversation or even to think about it. Instinctively, I said I was sure there was no one else like her.

"That's not what I'm saying, Laurence."

Now, four years and several appearances by her spirit later, I knew she was right. I wondered whether I would have had the foresight and grace to say this if things had been the other way round. She understood – and sometimes reminded me – that life is to be lived in the moment, and that it is more meaningful when life is lived with a partner.

As Richard and I strolled towards a tea shop, a final shadow caressed the sky, as the starlings wheeled away.

Melitta, in 1988, about a year after we met.

Melitta, circa 2001

The start, June 16, 2018. From left: Laura Holland (CRUK), Tanya Alevropoulos (my sister-in-law) and her husband Julian Borrill, my mother Barbara Carter, Margaret and Alan Miller (my mother's friends), me, and Jo Marriott (CRUK), in front of the Martello tower on the seafront at Seaford.

My friend Richard, my younger daughter Georgie, and me in front of the van.

My brother-in-law Julian, accompanying me on a wet day in Cornwall

A group of us ready to set off from Charlestown, Cornwall, where some of the Poldark series was filmed. From left: Me, Ana, Julia and Andy Gunther, David Donaldson, Kristin Brady, Luke Tetley, Nettie Alevropoulos-Borrill, a friend of Elizabeth Donaldson, Elizabeth, and Andrew Donaldson.

Sara Clancy (who, incredibly, turned out to be a close friend of the sister of Melitta's best friend at university), and Ian Mathieson, a close friend of mine, enjoying dinner after a tough day's walk.

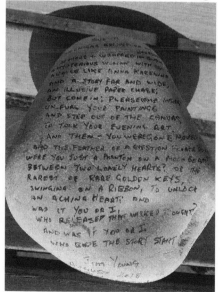

Mysterious poem left on a bench in Cornwall. I searched nearby for a woman with "a voice like Anna Karenina" without luck.

Phyllis (center, the mother of a work colleague), together with her friends Sheila and Pat, all aged between 73 and 84, guided me one day in the Gower peninsula, Wales. Would I like a walking stick so I could keep up, they teased? And who was I trying to impress with my map, they knew the route.

One of the hundred cast iron figures forming Antony Gormley's "Another Place" installation on Crosby beach, north of Liverpool. The figures, erected in 2005, are based on Gormley's body, and are spread over two miles.

Bas and Frederike Mohrmann among the snowdrops, near Hadrian's Wall.

Girl on a horse on a Lincolnshire beach, about to gallop through the surf again.

My Airbnb host, Simon, organized the community restoration of this Victorian-era fountain near his house in Hull. It had lain derelict since 1928.

East Nene lighthouse near The Wash, where Peter Scott lived for several years in the 1930s. Based on this experience, he founded the Wildlife and Wetlands Trust and later co-founded the World Wildlife Fund, serving as its first chairman, and designing WWF's iconic panda symbol.

My friend Paula enjoying a glass of wine after we had found Anne Boleyn's heart.

Last day, on Seaford Head, only a mile to go to the pub!

CHAPTER 16

LESSONS FROM THE EDGE

"When everyone is included, everyone wins." — Jesse Jackson.

Day 188, 20th December 2018, Holyhead, Isle of Anglesey, Wales 2,119 miles

A few days before Christmas, I was enjoying the hospitality of a boisterous family in Holyhead, on the northwest tip of the Isle of Anglesey, itself on the northwest extremity of Wales. Around the long, wooden kitchen table, illuminated by candles and laughter, a dozen people sat, ranging from four to sixty-four, a mix of the family, neighbours, and friends. Thursday was the family's weekly community evening. My hosts, 'David' and 'Alwen', a couple in their mid-forties, specialised in warm welcomes and cheerful parenting. I never worked out the number of progeny – six or seven would be a fair guess – all I know is that when I stumbled through in the morning, I passed little ones sleeping in nooks and crannies of the old house. David, who did not work because of a bad back, served as house husband, Airbnb host, and raconteur, while Alwen worked nine hours a day as a care home helper, and a further nine hours a day at home –

cooking, washing, reading to the children, and teasing her husband.

I arrived bedraggled after a damp, seventeen-mile hike around the western coast of Anglesey. A test of my resilience. A bridge to the island meant that it fitted my 'rule' of walking around land connected to the mainland, which in this case added 124 miles. However, the morning was entrancing; I discovered the tiny tidal island of Ynys Llanddwyn and a tale of unrequited love. For hundreds of years this desolate seventy-four-acre speck, reachable only at low tide, was a destination for pilgrims, because of Princess Dwynwen's sorrowful saga from 450 AD. She had fallen in love with a young man named Maelon, but her father had refused the marriage. Princess Dwynwen prayed to forget her love. An angel responded to Dwynwen's entreaties, providing her with a potion, which she duly passed to her lover. However, after Maelon drank the liquid, he turned into ice! Distraught, the princess retreated to Ynys Llanddwyn to build a church and to spend the rest of her life as a hermit. Later she was designated a saint, and her saint's day, 25 January, is celebrated in Wales as a day for lovers, rather than St. Valentine's Day. Captivated by this sad tale, and the lonely peace of the deserted tiny island, I tarried too long among the ruins of the princess' simple church and so stumbled the last few miles in the dark. David and Alwen's invitation to join their weekly get-together was perfect.

Picture Renoir's *Luncheon of the Boating Party*, but around a kitchen table, the dark of winter staved off by candlelight and the social energy. Animated conversations, spaghetti bolognese spilling off our plates and down the children's T-shirts, and wine glasses magically refilled. Into this melee, two young women suddenly appeared: David and Alwen's oldest daughter Rhiannon and her friend, Iona, home for the holidays. Upon finding out about my walk, Iona told her own story about how a doctor had turned her away at age twenty, saying no, screening tests only start at twenty-five.

I knew why, courtesy of Cancer Research UK. The chance of a false positive is higher before twenty-five, due to natural changes taking place in the cervix, so the National Health Service only starts screening then.

Iona continued, saying she asked to see another doctor, and that the test had been positive. Her takeaway: you must be assertive.

Everyone nodded in vigorous, wine-fuelled agreement, except for the five-year-old who asked her mother why she couldn't go to see the doctor too. The story resonated: my contact in Cancer Research UK, Jo, had told me that the 'gynae' cancers were socially where breast cancer was a generation earlier: a stigma, not for polite conversation.

Then, like walking out across rocky, seaweed-covered flats to a tidal island, danger suddenly appeared. David asked me what I thought of the Welsh coast path. I replied that I was impressed and had noticed the signs saying that the EU helped pay for the upgrading. Like the children's party game where everyone freezes the moment the music stops, the hubbub around the table ceased, with all eyes turning to David. Tension infused the atmosphere, the spring waiting to uncoil.

"We must get Brexit done," David said, grimly. "I don't trust those civil servants in London, they're trying to override the will of the people."

After a soliloquy about bureaucrats' devilment, David asked the gathering why we thought Brexit had happened. He continued, without waiting for an answer.

"Simple," said David. "It's not about Brussels regulating our bananas. Out here, *they've forgotten us*. They don't care about our schools, our bus services, our health centres. They wanted us to vote yes. But we told them to bugger off."

Nods of agreement from around the table, even the five-year-old.

David continued. "These civil servants in London, they're accountants. They cut our post offices, close our libraries, and reduce our bus services. In the summer, they visit, because their grannies live here, or so their children can play on the beach. Then they go back to their plush jobs and expensive houses, and everything is closed. The grannies watch TV alone all day because there are no buses, and the local post office has closed."

The evening had turned serious. What he said resonated: I had walked through those closed-up coastal towns. Luckily, one of the children let out an enormous burp at that moment. The tension lifted, and the jollity returned.

Later, I struggled to fall asleep. I was struck both by the warmth of the family and the depth of feelings about being abandoned by the government. But I had an underlying, more personal unease: if I was to learn to love again, I would need to learn to empathize again. This family was showing me the difference between analysing – in this case the reasons for Brexit – and *feeling*. Earlier in the walk I had learned from my hosts and companions to ask questions, to listen and to notice. I had reached base camp, but now I needed to start climbing. This evening was a start, forcing me to think from a different perspective. My education continued in the lonely far reaches of north-west England, in Cumbria.

THE NORTHWEST

JANUARY 10, 2018 – FEBRUARY 17, 2018, 483 MILES, 11,431 FEET OF CLIMB

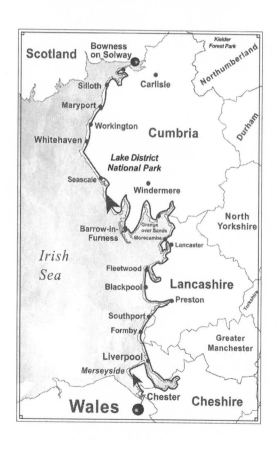

CHAPTER 17

MEANING

"The truth is, unless you let go, unless you forgive yourself, unless you forgive the situation, unless you realize that the situation is over, you cannot move forward." — Steve Maraboli.

Day 222, 23rd January 2019, Lytham St Annes, Lancashire, 2,451 miles

If the purpose of art is to transport us to a world of reflection and contemplation . . . success!

In early January, replete with the soul-searching memories inspired by Wales, I crossed the border back into England, near the old market town of Chester, circled the Wirral peninsula, and headed north. Some places surprised me. One afternoon, after passing Liverpool, as the sun's faint rays accentuated the dark edges of the clouds, I trekked along Crosby Beach, the site of Antony Gormley's *Another Place*: one hundred cast-iron sculptures of his own body, serenely staring out to the horizon, spread over two miles. The tide had receded, exposing the figures usually covered with water, still dripping, harbouring dark green strands of seaweed, gazing impassively seawards. No living being was in sight. I wandered from statue to statue, lost in thought, absently savouring the approaching sunset, and wondering what the future might hold.

I walked seawards across the mud flats to stand a few yards from the waves, wiping away a fleck of wave foam from my cap. Over the past seven months I'd walked nearly two thousand five hundred miles, so should be well over halfway by now, although it didn't appear that way on the map. I had under-estimated the distance around the English and Welsh coasts. The grey Irish sea a few yards away growled, poised to hurl a huge wave at any moment. A lone seagull swooped low over the restless water, cawing a plaintive *yeow* into the void. *Just you and me,* I whispered. The clouds hurried across the sky, ready to release more sleet into the mid-afternoon dusk. If I tarried too long, I would walk the last two miles in the dark. The sea's horizon was close, blurred by the haze of rain and wind-whipped white horses.

I fell back into a reverie to an evening about two years after Melitta and I had first met. By then we were living on the south Atlantic island of St Helena, where Napoleon had involuntarily resided and now where I was working as the government's economist. Melitta and I were engaged, but not yet married; our living together caused a minor scandal in the small society, still a British colony. We, together with another dozen people, had been invited to the Governor's mansion, Plantation House, for a dinner. The seating at the long table was strictly by hierarchy, so Melitta and I were placed at the other end from the Governor, enjoying ourselves with other young government employees. The scene could easily have been transposed back a hundred years; while the rest of Britain's empire had evaporated, stilted nineteenth-century traditions continued in this lonely outpost. Surrounded by portraits of former governors in the wood-panelled room, butlers served locally-caught fish, the Governor held forth, laughing at his own jokes, and the guests – mindful of the awkward formality of the occasion – tried to keep the conversation above the level of the usual island gossip. Then a pivotal moment arrived. The senior lady stood, announcing that she was moving next door. Chairs scraped on the old wooden floorboards as the other women rose. Melitta and the new doctor's wife sitting opposite – also in her mid-twenties – exchanged glances and surreptitious headshakes. They did not budge. The last woman to leave the room left the door ajar, an invitation to Melitta and her ally to respond. They sat there, implacable. The Governor glowered from his perch but said nothing. The shocked butler offered Melitta and her co-conspirator brandy and port, along with the men. And the chatter of conversation resumed. Another tiny advance towards the twentieth century.

Looking out over the Irish Sea, I felt a tiny crab scrabble up my bare shins, perhaps surprised at its change of terrain from grey pebbles. I sensed that change loomed for me too, beyond the geographical milestone. It had been three and a half years since Melitta passed away. I was beginning to look ahead, lurching into uncharted territory. What would happen in five months, after my walk around England and Wales finished? *What would you have done, Meloo? But you're not here, at least not physically, and you're never going to be again. This is on me.* I glanced behind at the empty land, an impassive mixture of grassy tussocks and rocks, adapted to millennia of wind and rain. And back at the churning sea. We need to do both, I mused: honour the past, and those we loved, and prepare for what fate will throw our way. All we can control is our outlook and effort. The seagull careened across the sky, carefree, scanning the roiling waves. The crab perched on my knee, enjoying the view.

A day or two later I arrived in Lytham St Annes in south Lancashire on a bitterly cold afternoon, clapping my gloves together to keep the circulation going. It would have been warmer if it had been snowing, but instead there was simply a strong breeze blowing flecks of wave foam onto the muddy path, which had started to glaze over. My knowledge of the town was limited to knowing it had a famous golf course; I was about to discover something more interesting. I knocked on the door of my host for the next two nights, Dee Cartledge.

A genial, busy woman a few years younger than me, Dee radiated a brusque kindness, which she deployed within ten minutes of my arrival. The kettle was about to boil when I stepped out of the back door to knock the frozen mud off my boots and, suddenly I was airborne, almost horizontal, like an ungainly mid-air picture of a judo player. I landed on the ice flat on my back with a loud thwack. I was more embarrassed than hurt, but Dee insisted on cooking me dinner to help me recover. The mug of tea was soon replaced by a wine glass. She told me her partner ran a restaurant; I asked when he would arrive home. She laughed uproariously:

"Oh no, I couldn't possibly live with him. It's great seeing him each week and going on holiday, though."

The phone rang for the third time since I had arrived.

"You are one busy lady," I said.

"Yeah, it's my foundation," Dee explained.

"Foundation?" I queried. "Tell me more."

"It's a long story, which I don't usually tell my guests. But if you're ready to listen . . ." She broke off, looking pensive.

I sensed the change in mood and sat quietly.

Twenty years earlier, Dee was living an everyday life with two grown sons and a husband. Her elder son, then aged twenty-three, who lived 100 miles away, called her excitedly to tell her about a job interview. She rang him the next day to ask how it went; his voice sounded strange. Her younger son, who lived near his elder brother, told her that his brother had the flu. The next day her younger son called again, hysterical, saying the ambulance had arrived to take his brother to hospital. A few minutes later, the hospital phoned to tell her that her son had died – from 'necrotising fasciitis.' Dee explained to me that this meant that part of the fascia – the tissue surrounding every organ, bone, nerve, and muscle in the body had been killed by bacteria. Known colloquially as 'flesh-eating disease', it can develop after a cut, bruise, or sore throat. In her son's case, infection from a tooth abscess had spread into his internal organs, and gangrene had developed. Dee went on to explain that NF is rare and curable with antibiotics but must be treated quickly, as it moves so fast through the body.

Dee's world fell apart – and that wasn't the end. Her distraught husband committed suicide a few months later. And her remaining son suffered from PTSD after seeing his brother die.

Dee said that she grieved for some months, but then she decided she needed to do something to make a difference. She set up the UK's only organisation dedicated to raising awareness about the disease, the Lee Spark NF Foundation. All of this had happened twenty years earlier and since then Dee and her team had run sessions for thousands of schoolchildren and medical professionals around how to recognise the warning signs of NF.

I sat, open-mouthed. The last of the spaghetti bolognese on my plate lay untouched, as I idly swirled the wine. Dee's voice was clear and firm, answering my unspoken question.

"Had to look forward. I couldn't bear stewing on all that tragedy. Had to do something, it's given me meaning. Well, you know, 'cos you're doing something similar."

Except I wasn't really. I mulled the difference. This jovial, no-nonsense woman had mustered inner strength to build a non-profit to raise awareness, sustaining the effort for years. She had turned tragedy into a vision and executed it day in day out. My walk was just a temporary effort. The next day, heading north towards Blackpool, I thought about her insight: true meaning comes from looking forwards, even if it is rooted in past tragedy. How could I apply that, I wondered?

CHAPTER 18

MESSING UP

"White privilege is about the word white, not rich. It's having advantage built into your life. It's not saying your life hasn't been hard; it's saying your skin colour hasn't contributed to the difficulty in your life." — Emmanuel Acho.

Day 235, 5th February 2019, Seascale, Cumbria, 2,625 miles

At the onset of February, I began walking along Cumbria's remote coast. One evening stood out. My host was a glum woman in her early sixties. She had moved to the northwest twenty years earlier, following her husband, who had later left to pursue another woman. After introductory pleasantries, including mention of a feud with her neighbour, she announced:

"You know, they're all in-bred around here. Cousins and all that."

I wasn't sure how to reply, so I asked about the Wi-Fi instead. But there was no stopping her.

"No one smiles," she grimaced. "They don't like outsiders. They need fresh genes."

This was the strangest opening conversation I had faced. I

thought about asking her why she continued to live among these supposedly gene-limited people but instead asked her who stayed with her in the winter. My host had converted the three bedrooms in her house for Airbnb guests while she slept on a couch in the living room. The facilities were spartan, but the cost was low, so the rooms were usually booked.

"Contractors working at the nuclear power station, health workers, reps, and the odd person like you," she said, half-smiling. "You're a bit odder than most. I have my regulars. But don't park in front of the neighbour's house."

She returned to her pet theme of poor genetic diversity, almost in a stream of consciousness. When we reached the bathroom, she picked up the scales and placed them on the toilet cistern.

"You can't use those; they belong to Heike. She'll be back tonight. Haven't told you about Heike, have I? Wait till you meet her, she is something else." My landlady laughed mirthlessly. "Ah, Heike, she's a foreigner. Just what they need to spice things up. But she's too exotic for the locals. She's Croatian, she's Black, and she's a bodybuilder and a physician. She's based in Dundee, but the National Health Service sends her here three days a week. I doubt if her patients understand a word she says. You'll see."

I was intrigued. I'd never met a Black Croatian bodybuilding medic before. I settled down with a beer, the newspaper, and my usual assortment from the supermarket – bread, cheese, olives, celery, and a squishy jam doughnut. No prizes for diet, but fifteen miles of trekking through soggy fields meant it didn't matter.

Then Heike arrived, bursting through the old wooden door, and filling the room with energy.

"So, you are the man-in-shorts?" she grinned. Heike's Slavic accent was perfectly understandable.

Although broad-shouldered, she didn't remind me of the

bodybuilders I'd seen on TV. Her open face and wide smile suggested that she engaged actively with the world, welcoming sociability. She said she'd heard me on the radio that afternoon and figured I must be crazy. Heike's next query threw me.

"So, man-in-shorts, guess how old I am!"

This was treacherous territory. I had only just finished navigating tales of inbreeding neighbours. A quick scan suggested that she might be in her forties.

"Hmm, I'd guess you're mid-thirties, Heike?" I ventured politely.

Heike chuckled, saying she would tell me a secret.

"You know what, walker-man, I'm nearly as old as . . . you! I know your age from the radio interview." She chortled, cascading into a crescendo of peals of laughter. "I'm fifty-three, but you wouldn't believe it, would you?"

I was astonished and told her so. I pushed the bread and cheese aside and asked her to join me for a beer. Over several drinks, she told me her life story. Twenty years earlier, she moved with a boyfriend from Croatia to London. After the boyfriend left, she had stayed, finding the city more hospitable for her skin colour than Croatia. Eventually, she ended up in Dundee; she wasn't sure how, although we were on our third beer by then.

Another boyfriend had suggested that she try bodybuilding so that they could work out together. Heike had agreed and much to her astonishment, she started winning local bodybuilding competitions. This proved too much for her partner, who left, intimidated by his more successful companion. Heike confided that she was lonely, although she had friends in Dundee and Cumbria. Shuttling back and forth weekly was tough on her social life. I asked whether there were any possibilities among the men in the bodybuilding community. Heike laughed, wrinkling the creases around her eyes as she raised her eyebrows.

"They're all too busy looking at themselves in the mirror."

She turned serious and told me she was tired of being the only Black person in the clinic. Sometimes her patients asked where the doctor or nurse was, thinking she was the cleaner. She stated, matter-of-factly, that I had no idea what this was like and would not understand. I nodded, knowing she was right. But, she said, it was draining. When I asked her whether she'd thought about relocating back to London, she asked why she should always be the one to adjust. Besides, she preferred Scotland and northern England – the people were friendlier and more plainspoken.

"As a white man, you can go anywhere and you don't have to think. As a woman, I need to be careful, and as a black woman, I won't always be welcome. That's the way it is. But it doesn't have to be."

As we bade each other goodnight, I felt ashamed that I had focused on the identity markers before meeting this hard-working, friendly professional woman who was easy to talk to, wanted people to accept her skin colour, and yearned for a life partner. My lessons in building empathy were continuing. But simultaneously, I was messing up.

I knew that I was beginning to be attracted to women again. But I was creating some awkward situations. In early February I called my emotional adviser, my elder daughter Emily.

"I need advice. Remember I told you I walked a few months ago with a lady called Rebecca for a few days? Someone I didn't know before. Well, I think I messed up and sent the wrong signals. She's returning to walk with me again next week."

"What's wrong with that?" said Emily. "Very nice of her."

"True," I said, "but she has booked a hotel room for us. Together. But I'm not ready for that. I don't want to upset her. What should I do?"

"Hmm, Dad, tell her exactly that. That you aren't ready for any relationships yet. You're looking forward to walking with her, but you think it would be better to stay separately. Oh, and you know what?"

"What?" I asked.

"That day, it's Valentine's Day. Don't mess her around."

I took Emily's sage advice and enjoyed the few days with Rebecca. Still, I realised that I needed once again to master the knack of navigating relationships. I was ready in principle but struggled with opening the gate.

Timing is everything!

HADRIAN'S WALL AND NORTHUMBERLAND

FEBRUARY 17, 2019 – MARCH 4, 2019
195 MILES, 9,726 FEET OF CLIMB

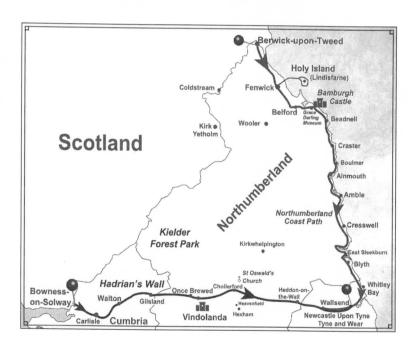

CHAPTER 19

BOUNDARIES

"Men build too many walls and not enough bridges." — Joseph
Fort Newton.

**Day 242, 12th February 2019, Whitehaven, Cumbria, 2,724
miles**

S everal months before I had set off, my CRUK contact, Jo,
had proposed that I scale back ambition and traverse the
country via Hadrian's Wall, which stretches seventy-three miles
from Bowness-on-Solway in the west to Wallsend on the east
coast. I had demurred, explaining that I couldn't reappear at
work again after a week. Nevertheless, the conversation stuck,
and I chose the Hadrian's Wall path instead of tracking the
actual England-Scotland border, which ran further north. Still,
to ensure that I covered every yard of the English coast, I would
divert north once I reached the end of the wall in Newcastle.

Fast forward to January 2019, when I was heading north on
the Cumbrian coast, still seventy miles from where I would turn
east along the wall's path. On a remote stretch of coast, bereft of
human habitation, and on a day when the sleet was particularly

horizontal, the pubs were noticeably closed, and my bare legs were decidedly cold, I stumbled upon a lonely farmhouse brandishing an astonishing sign: '*Afternoon Tea*'. Forlornly I knocked, certain it was left over from the summer. The door opened, and an angel dressed as a beaming man welcomed me into a warm room with a log fire and a hint of freshly baked bread in the air.

"Come in and dry off. You look like you could use a cuppa."

This could not be real! Unsurprisingly, I was the only customer that day and probably the whole week. Tea, buttered crumpets, homemade jam, dollops of cream…I asked the host why he stayed open in the winter. He was a genial man in his sixties, with a weather-beaten face and a demeanour that rolled with the punches of life.

"Oh, there's often an oddball or two coming through. Like you. I enjoy hearing people's stories. The farm doesn't pay for itself any longer. We're going to sell, but I like it out here."

We chatted as I dried out. He had popped back into the kitchen to refill the teapot when my phone buzzed with an email:

I'm currently in The Netherlands and today the wind is blowing particularly hard and wet from the west… I can only imagine the hardship at the UK coast, along with the enjoyment when entering a warm, dry inn for a hot drink or good meal. Frederike and I would like to join you for a week in February or March…Bas

Bas and I had worked together in Washington for years. A tall, good-humoured Dutch agricultural specialist, who kept a twinkle in his eye and rustled up marvellous stories, Bas had retired a few months before I started the walk. At his farewell party, he had mentioned that he was interested in joining, but I thought no more of it then.

I emailed back to Bas with some dates in February and asked my host for the bill. He waved away that insolent request and stepped outside to guide me. The clouds were scudding across the sky and tumbling over the horizon. A long, ominous dusk was beginning at 3 p.m. I stumbled along the boulder-strewn beach, marvelling at the seaweed, relishing the boundary of stormy sea and dim light: sea lettuce, gutweed, bladderwrack, and purple laver. Quite a coincidence, I mused: the kindness of a stranger and the generosity of a work colleague.

Ten days later, Bas and Frederike joined in Carlisle on the second leg of the Hadrian's Wall route. They hadn't missed any stonework: the previous day's walk from the official starting point on the west coast, Bowness-on-Solway, had not contained any hint of remaining wall, apart from a sign announcing that Wallsend was eighty-four miles away. Wallsend was originally named Segedunum until the locals decided it was a mouthful. Once we started climbing up into the hills, heading towards the intriguingly named hamlet of Once Brewed, we began seeing remnants of the wall. As the land emptied itself of human habitation, the traces turned into intact sections of the 1,900-year-old wall, up to fifteen feet high and ten feet wide. It was eerie, following the same path trodden by the Roman centurions, surveying the hills they gazed upon, no doubt dreaming of Tuscany.

Bas and Frederike exuded contentment. The smorgasbord of historical nuggets, rolling countryside, fresh air, pubs, and conversation felt right. Frederike, a smiling, average-sized woman who appeared short next to Bas, had the stride of a Roman centurion. I marvelled at the richness of their relationship. Frederike said she started long ago laughing at Bas's bad jokes and now found them funny after years of practice. I remembered, wistfully, occasions when Melitta had said something funny; I'd laughed, then she'd started giggling, which set me off again, unable to stop. The children would look at us, bemused and horrified at their parents' behaviour. Ah, what I would give to re-live one of those moments. Bas and Frederike recognised that one secret to a rich marriage is for each partner to give – attention, encouragement, kindness, laughter – while allowing the other to remain their own person.

I was impressed with Bas's three-part planning for retirement. First, he would look for fulfilling work – he was helping an Indian company create a university to teach sustainable irrigation and organic farming. Another third of the time was engaging with family, friends, and community – hence their decision to join me. Indeed, Bas and Frederike had turned the week into a veritable community effort, securing sponsorship from dozens of friends and updating them each evening. The final third of Bas's time was personal – exercising, reading, meditating, and upgrading their house. I asked how reality had panned out.

"Well, Laurence, one part worked well. Frederike and I are reconnecting with people and making new friends." Bas paused, surveying the surrounding green hills from his great height. "The problem is that I love the work. So, I've put more than a third of my time into that and struggled to exercise, read and fix the house."

In his gentle, self-deprecating way, Bas said it was too early to judge, and, by the way, wasn't that the pub marking the end of the day's stroll? Indeed, there was the *Twice Brewed* inn, replete with a blazing fire, warm ale, and rich soup, perfect for weary walkers along Hadrian's Wall – of whom there were no others on that blustery, showery day. Reputedly, the inn was so-called because eighteenth-century farmers used to brew weak ale for themselves, so 'twice brewed' signalled that the hostelry offered stronger beer. Nearby was the first youth hostel in England, built in 1934. A Lady Trevelyan of Wallington Hall, a fierce teetotaller, gave the opening speech, referring to the nearby inn and saying, "Of course, there will be no alcohol served on these premises, so I hope the tea and coffee will only be brewed once." Thus, the youth hostel and nearby houses became 'Once Brewed'. We warmed our hands over the fire, supped our ale and soup, agreed that most of the famous walls in history had failed to keep people out – and that everyone celebrates when they are torn down. Replete and fortified, we stumbled back outside, thanking Hadrian for bestowing us with the stones to build the pub. As we left, I heard Frederike chortle again and asked her what Bas had said.

"I'm not really sure, the wind is a bit noisy," she smiled, "but he just makes me laugh."

I nodded, knowing that was what I was missing.

CHAPTER 20

SAINTS

"I am not a saint unless you think of a saint as a sinner who keeps on trying." — Nelson Mandela.

Day 252, 22nd February 2019, Chollerford, Northumberland, 2,847 miles

Day five of the Hadrian's Wall hike. Frederike, Bas, and I set off with a spring in our step. The weather gods had swept away the rain and wind of the previous days to reveal a pristine winter morning, with the sun glinting on the frost coating the leaves and grass. Our boots crunched the frozen leaves and our breath swirled in the still air. Despite the cold, the bright light hinted at a warmth to come, and there was a palpable feeling of nature stirring.

We had been treated to a grand stay by our host, 'Miranda', a friendly woman overlain with the manners of a lady-of-the-manor. She had greeted us the evening before with a homemade lemon cake and tea, which felt completely decadent after a blustery, sixteen-mile walk. Miranda lived in a house built by a knight in 1300s –no doubt using stones from Hadrian's Wall.

That evening, fortified by shepherd's pie and Yorkshire ale, Bas and Frederike slept in a four-poster bed in the fourteenth-century tower. They enjoyed themselves searching for graffiti left by the noble chevaliers who had inhabited the room five hundred years earlier.

Before we arrived, Miranda emailed to tell me that my room would be free as her contribution to the walk. My hosts often exhibited such touching kindness, including sometimes cooking a special dinner. The following morning Miranda prepared a breakfast that a gourmet hotel would struggle to match. The fruit platter alone was a designer piece of art which could have graced the Tate Modern. The three of us tucked in, turning it into an art experience. There followed scrambled eggs, crackly bacon, organic mushrooms, a wedge of tomato, a dollop of spinach, a slice of black pudding, and coffee. We could barely manage the colour-coordinated granola, berries, and yoghurt to finish the feast.

The morning path wended into woods, a welcome change from the past two days of traipsing over treeless hillsides. The gnarled trunks of the oaks hinted at ages past, springy moss covered the shaded part of the slopes, and roots curled across the trail. As we strode deeper among the trees, we spotted ivy clinging to branches and heard the birds chattering as they searched for nesting places. A woodpecker was busy knocking on the door of spring. Life was emerging from winter hibernation in an ancient forest, as it had done for hundreds of years. Suddenly, one of those moments happened that you cannot anticipate and will never forget. The gods had been busy. We chanced upon a magical vista of tens of thousands of the first flower of spring – snowdrops, daintily announcing nature's renewal. The gods, or fairies, had not so much sprinkled them throughout the primaeval land as poured them out wholesale.

We gazed in awe, savouring the evanescent miracle. Such

moments are best shared. I hoped that Melitta's spirit was among us; she would have relished this wonder of nature with the gusto of a medieval monk tucking into his first flagon of mead after a long day of chanting and praying. I sighed inwardly, missing her more than usual. Frederike, Bas, and I tarried among the delicate white flowers, marvelling at the spectacle. This was a prelude to another surprise.

At first sight, the church on the Hadrian's Wall path, St. Oswald's, appeared to be normal. Then Frederike called me over, saying the story was straight out of *Game of Thrones*. In AD 633, King Oswald fought King Cadwallon of Gwynedd, Wales, who had invaded Northumbria. The armies met at Heavenfield, near the village of Hexham. Oswald, who was a Christian, erected a wooden cross the day before the battle. The Welsh army was routed and Oswald commemorated the victory by building a church and appointing an Irish bishop, Aidan, to spread the word.

One Easter, Oswald and Aidan were feasting when a servant announced that the poor were begging for crumbs. The King sent dishes of venison and wild boar outside. Impressed with this generosity, Aidan grabbed Oswald's hand, saying, "May this hand never perish." Reputedly, after Oswald was killed in battle a few years later, his severed arm did not decay and became a sought-after relic. The miracle of Oswald's 'uncorrupted' arm, plus his role as a winner writing history, meant he became Saint Oswald and pilgrims starting visiting Heavenfield.

Bas, Frederike, and I wandered around St. Oswald's church and cemetery, the ancient battle site, absorbing the atmosphere. Who has ever heard of Heavenfield, or even Oswald, unless you live in Northumberland? We were alone; indeed, we saw no other walkers that day. When we continued, Hadrian's Wall path also became St. Oswald's Way. It felt special to be traipsing in the footsteps of medieval pilgrims.

Two days later, after we had completed the Hadrian's Wall stretch and Bas and Frederike had departed, I drove up to Berwick-upon-Tweed, at the Scottish border, ready to start walking south down the Northumberland coast. Soon, I encountered St. Cuthbert's Way, named after a monk born in 634, the year St. Oswald defeated the Welsh interloper, Cadwallon. Multiple saints were strolling the Northumbria countryside in those days! Cuthbert lived the traditional life of a trainee saint, initially serving in a monastery and then wandering as a hermit for years, preaching, performing miracles, and ending as bishop of Holy Island in 684. St. Cuthbert became the most popular saint in England for several hundred years until the murder of Thomas Becket in Canterbury in 1170.

The Middle Ages were the peak pilgrimage period. Nowadays, we associate the idea of a pilgrimage with a long journey. But medieval pilgrims could not afford to travel to distant lands, so they visited a local shrine to ask for forgiveness, health, or luck with finding the right partner. Churches competed to host saintly remains and promote miracles. When St. Oswald was killed, his body was chopped into pieces, allowing multiple churches around England and Europe to claim his remains. Oswald's arm resided for years at Bamburgh Castle on Northumberland's coast until an enterprising monk from Peterborough Abbey stole it in a midnight raid. The pilgrims duly re-routed. However, Henry VIII ruined the whole saint-relic-pilgrim business with his dissolution of the monasteries in the 1530s. St. Oswald's uncorrupted arm disappeared from the abbey at Peterborough, never to be seen again.

One day, as I walked south along the wild, best-kept-secret of Northumberland's coast, I sought out a café and googled St. Oswald's Way and St. Cuthbert's Way. Surprise: it was all in the branding! The 62-mile St. Cuthbert's Way was launched in 1996, and the 97-mile St. Oswald's Way was announced a decade later, in 2006. All that time, I had imagined those holy men 1,400 years earlier, treading on the same turf, navigating the treacherous tidal route to Lindisfarne, planning their campaign of converting the local heathens. Recreational walkers are the modern pilgrims, after all.

As I approached the three-thousandth mile, my thoughts turned from saints to the prosaic as I noticed a toe protruding from the side of my shoe, like a giant wart. It was time to change my boots again.

THE NORTHEAST

**MARCH 5, 2019 – APRIL 1, 2019,
307 MILES, 12,778 FEET OF CLIMB**

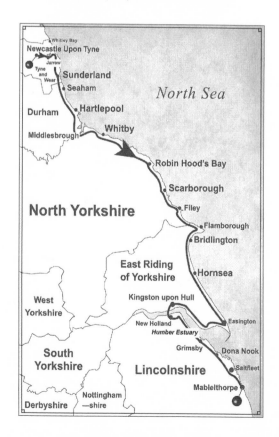

CHAPTER 21

FURTHER TO GO

"In three words, I can sum up everything I've learned about life: it goes on." — Robert Frost.

Day 264, 6th March 2019, Seaham, Durham, 3,009 miles

I passed the three-thousand-mile mark on a windy, cloudy March 6th, somewhere between Jarrow and Seaham on the Durham coast. Pausing for a few minutes of reflection on the milestone, I sat on a bench that had a memorable remembrance line for a couple:

'They lived for those they loved,
And those they loved, remember.'

Can't ask for much more than that, I thought, inhaling the fresh, salty air. I stretched out on the bench, head resting on my backpack, to shelter from the wind and with the hope of slipping into a meditative state.

My thoughts strayed toward the future. By now, it was clear that my original estimate of 3,500 miles was too optimistic. There was most of eastern England to go, plus the Essex creeks, turning west into London to cross the Thames and then heading south back to Seaford, including a shimmy around the Isle of Grain off the Kent coast. The final tally would be well over four thousand miles. But I still had to finish in late June as I was due back at work in July. A hundred days left, with over thirteen hundred miles to go. Hmm, I would need to speed up on those long Lincolnshire stretches.

Eyes closed, relaxed on the bench, listening to the surf and the whine of the wind, I took stock. Nearly nine months in, how was it going? Physically, all was good—I had lost ten pounds, despite supping too many pints of ale. Socially: great. Many friends had joined, and the Airbnb hosts were often quirky and kind. Jo, from Cancer Research UK, was pleased too. Since Jackie had started guiding me in November, like a pilot through a marshy channel, awareness-raising had taken off, particularly with local radio and newspapers. Fundraising was ticking along, especially after Jo set up a text number for donations.

My journey to better self-awareness was messier. 'Cafeteria-man' had been right to predict that I would be affected by those I met along the way. The contrast between this experience, involving multiple touchpoints with new people every day, often at a surprisingly personal level, with the repetitive routines of 'normal life' was stark. There had been such a goulash of influences, however, that I wasn't sure how the final dish would turn out. My first Airbnb host, Tim the Toast, had encouraged me to ask the right questions, although I was still working out what they were. I had learned to listen and notice more and in return had been treated to some extraordinary and sometimes tragic stories. Sara had spotted my weakness with outreach and had prodded me to find someone to help; if I had waited to figure this out myself, I would still be struggling. The conversation with Heike the black Croatian bodybuilder had reminded me to stay open-minded – and to try harder to put myself in other peoples' shoes. Perhaps my biggest surprise about myself was embracing unusual coincidences and feeling that Melitta's spirit was accompanying me on this journey. Overall, my self-awareness antennae were up, messages were being received, but I wasn't sure how to interpret all the signals.

Emotionally, however, I was flailing. I sensed that I was ready to learn to love again. I had found the host who had been defrauded attractive, seeing the Cornish couple teasing each other was joyous and envy-inducing, like watching dolphins jumping through waves, and Bas and Frederike's deep contentment with each other was inspiring. But I had unwittingly sent ambiguous signals to one of my co-walkers, 'Rebecca'. And the temporary nature of the journey, which involved meeting people for a day or two, was not conducive to developing relationships anyway. No evident pathway on that front. Maybe best not to overthink it anyway; my daughter Emily's advice about 'doing what feels right' always seemed spot on. But there was something else.

I shifted on the bench, covered my face with my woollen ski cap, and tried to concentrate. A thought had been niggling away in my semi-conscious. I remembered an incident from August when my brother-in-law Julian and I were walking together. On a glorious sunny day, we were hiking a hilly stretch of the south Cornish coast near Looe. We were climbing a set of steps on the coast path, and our chatting had subsided to 'I-thought-I-was-fitter-than-this' laboured breathing. We stopped halfway up, ostensibly to admire the view, but really to recover. A well-aged woman was stepping down with a spring in her step, a light stick for balance, and deep laugh lines around her eyes. In her early eighties, I guessed.

She brushed a wisp of grey hair away and asked: "Hello, gentlemen, do you know how far it is to Whitsand Bay?"

"Well, we started from there, say three miles," we gasped.

"Ah, great, this is my last leg. On the South West Coast Path."

Julian and I glanced at each other. An 80-year-old walking 630 miles and climbing thousands of feet? She explained matter-of-factly. When she turned seventy-five, she resolved to show her granddaughters that it was possible to achieve anything if you put your mind to it. So, she set a goal of walking the 630-mile trail, covering around 100 miles each summer. She aimed to finish in six years but had taken a year off. We asked her why.

"Well, a relative needed a kidney, so I gave him mine."

Eighty-two years old, walking the South West Coast Path, with one kidney, for her grandchildren! Julian and I bid her fair speed, lost in admiration, dabbed with humble pie.

I pondered this story, as well as Dee Cartledge's initiative to set up a foundation in honour of her son. Both women had derived meaning by doing something practical for future generations.

A splat of seagull poop landing on the weathered arm of the bench jerked me out of my reverie.

Enough self-reflection.

I struggled up, pulled my woollen cap over my ears, hitched the backpack up and studied the map. I had further to go.

CHAPTER 22

LIVING AND LOVING

"True, we love life, not because we are used to living, but because we are used to loving. There is always some madness in love, but there is also always some reason in madness." — Petrarch.

Day 271, 13th March 2019, Saltburn-by-Sea, North Yorkshire, 3,080 miles

I was sitting in the kitchen of a Yorkshire Airbnb, devouring a mouth-watering breakfast of scrambled eggs, mushrooms, tomato, and an unknown vegetarian substance, when 'Ruth', my host, appeared by the doorframe.

"May I join you?" she asked with a shy smile.

She was leaning against the kitchen doorframe, with the sunlight splashing brightly across the countertops, lighting up her face. Her wan smile suggested she had seen more than her fair share of sorrow. Ruth, a good-looking woman, had a steady gaze and carried herself with a carefree air but nonetheless appeared a little shy. I guessed she was a similar age to me, but my record on this front was lousy. Laugh lines caressed her cheeks and twinkled around her eyes.

"Of course, I'd be delighted," I said.

Ruth's terraced house, in a seaside village on the Yorkshire coast, was decorated with a nautical theme. A few inches from my ear, a fishing net hung from the ceiling, painted in wavy shades of turquoise and aquamarine. Seashells festooned most surfaces. A thick seafarer's rope was entwined around the bannisters. Pieces of driftwood were artfully placed. A glass buoy served as a lampshade. I kept a close eye out for stray fishing hooks. If one listened carefully, the soothing sound of the late winter waves crashing onto the beach two hundred yards away was audible. But today, the sunshine was accompanied by a blustery wind, insistently rattling the gutters and windowpanes, so the sea was almost drowned out. A day to procrastinate, dawdle indoors, and postpone the fateful moment of stepping outside into the flying gutters and salty spray. Ruth wiped her hands on her apron, moved a sea urchin from the table, and sat beside me.

Things started quietly. Ruth poured a cup of tea and sat still, glancing my way. That felt awkward, so I broke the silence by asking about the picture above the fireplace. Unlike most items in the room, it had no nautical link: it was a painting of a baobab tree.

"Oh, I lived as a child in Botswana, and that painting is of a famous baobab which was nearby," said Ruth, smiling at the memory.

"That's a coincidence," I replied, "I worked in Botswana in my twenties. Where did you live?"

I expected her to name the capital city, Gaborone. Although Botswana is the size of France, its population is less than 2.5 million people – mostly living on the edges of the Kalahari Desert. I was so astonished by her answer that I almost choked on the vegetarian delicacy.

"A tiny village called Pandamatenga," she answered. "My

father was an irrigation engineer there in the late 1950s. It's in the north."

"Good grief, that's incredible," I exclaimed. Melitta's spirit was at work again, fostering connections.

I knew Pandamatenga, but only because I worked as a road planner for the government in the 1980s. I remembered it as having around thirty dwellings and a shop. A place where you wondered why people had settled there. And why they stayed. There could not be more than a few dozen people in the UK who knew of Pandamatenga; this was like asking a person from Botswana if they had heard of the Northumbrian village of Twice Brewed.

Ruth had grown up there. Life was quiet, unsurprisingly. We talked about the nearby baobab tree where Livingstone had camped en route to "discovering" Victoria Falls in 1855. Or, more accurately, bringing Victoria Falls to the attention of Europeans and giving Mosi-wa-Tunya – the Smoke that Thunders – a new name. One day, Ruth remembered, a bedraggled white man emerged from the nearby Kalahari Desert and stayed for some time. Upon hearing that her mother was a typist, he asked her to type a manuscript he had written.

"Laurens van der Post," she said, "and the book was *The Lost World of the Kalahari*. Have you heard of him?"

Another double-take! Although Laurens van der Post, a South African writer and the godfather of Prince William, is now as dated as fax machines, he was well-known in the 1970s. His books were suffused with a mystical lyricism – and later much criticised. *The Lost World of the Kalahari* was his most famous book. I envisaged a shaggy-bearded man stumbling out of the nearby salt pans into Pandamatenga, having his first cold drink in months, chatting to the family on the veranda, and pulling a hand-written manuscript from his backpack.

Unexpectedly, our conversation took a more personal turn.

155

Perhaps the reminiscing had made Ruth wistful. I asked her whether she had more guests coming in the next few days, and she said no, she was going on a retreat. She needed to think.

Ruth took me on a journey along the contours of her life. The family had returned to England in the 1960s, and Ruth had married young. A fine marriage, she said, and she and her husband had a baby girl. Now her grown daughter lived in Australia, she mentioned.

One day, after twenty-five years of marriage, her husband announced that he was leaving, as he had fallen in love. He had focused his attentions on the daughter of Ruth's closest friend, whom the family had known since birth. A 25-year age difference. Outside, a fierce gust of wind rattled the gutters, as if empathising with this cruel, unpredictable turn in life's path. Ruth, however, was determined not to be a hapless victim and signed up with Volunteer Service Overseas. A few months later, by then in her late forties, she headed to Vietnam to teach English. Then her life transformed once more. Entranced, I asked her what happened.

"Love," she answered simply.

She hadn't been searching, she stressed. She and a French teacher fell profoundly in love. She explained that it felt deeper than when she met her first husband in her late teens. They married in Vietnam and returned three years later to live in England. In due course, though, her husband announced that he was not impressed with the English and could not bear the weather. Glancing outside at the clothes straining horizontally on the line, I felt he might have had a point. They decamped to France.

Life was bliss, Ruth said, for ten years. She repeated the word quietly, in gratitude. One day, her husband announced, I'm sorry, I've fallen in love with someone else. A woman twenty-five years younger than him, in her late 30s. She waited, hoping that it was a phase.

"I loved that man," she repeated, almost to herself.

The two of us sat in silence. The infatuation phase for Ruth's husband outlasted her willingness to suffer continued humiliation. So she returned to the gales, gossip, and ennui of the village in northeast England, chastened by the men she had loved, who had both chased young women. That was ten years earlier, and she had taken up Airbnb to make ends meet and encounter new people. But now it was time to ponder what to embark upon next and how she might find a partner for her remaining years.

"Another pot of tea?" she asked brightly, lifting the pensive mood.

Ruth bustled in the kitchen, while the tea brewed. The bright sunlight hinted at the onset of spring despite the moaning gale. This amazing woman picked herself up from life's vicissitudes, time and again, expressing no self-pity. Instead, she emphasised that she had experienced love. Her spirit was infectious. And her openness to sharing vulnerability – perhaps stimulated by our mutual connection to Botswana. If I lived in this little town, I would have sought to meet her again.

CHAPTER 23

CONNECTIONS

"In nature, we never see anything isolated, but everything in connection with something else which is before it, beside it, under it and over it." — Johann Wolfgang von Goethe.

Day 277, 19th March 2019, Scarborough, North Yorkshire, 3,117 miles

I arrived at Scarborough's Harbour Bar after putting eight miles on my Strava app, ready for refreshment. Along the way, I'd read on my phone that you'll live an extra nine years if you can stand up from sitting on the ground without leaning on an arm or leg. I glanced around the Harbour Bar for a spot to try, but it didn't look feasible. Later, I confirmed that this is impossible for those of us who don't engage in extreme yoga.

I had just started to tuck into a knickerbocker glory when my phone beeped. *Where are you?*

It was from Chris, a guy I knew from a Facebook group of fifteen people circumnavigating the UK. I had kept quiet in the group because I felt like a fraud. Most participants were 'wild camping', in contrast to my Airbnbs and warm showers. The exchanges included techniques for drying out wet sleeping bags and lightening backpacks – for example by sawing handles off toothbrushes. Unlike most people, Chris and his dog Moose were walking anti-clockwise. We had corresponded a few times, perhaps once a month. I'd enjoyed his video posts, which made the mudflats of Essex sound downright gory.

Chris, I'm in Scarborough, where are you? I replied. I nearly swallowed a chemically red cherry whole when he answered: *Hi mate, I've just arrived in Scarborough too. Meet up? Give me a couple of hours to soak in a bath, first one for three weeks.*

What were the chances? I was walking clockwise, so we would have crossed somewhere, but for him to message me during my one hour in the whole year in Scarborough...well, I was used to serendipity by now.

We met that afternoon in the lobby of the Travelodge, where Chris and Moose were recovering after several weeks of wild camping. Like me, he started in June 2018. He was raising funds for a UK housing NGO, *Shelter*, and the mysteriously titled charity *Bras Not Bombs*. Chris and I were both thirsty, so the first glass rapidly became the second. He had completed around two thousand miles together with his enormous, friendly dog, Moose. Chris, an easy-to-smile man in his early forties, an engineer, explained that he wanted a change from the humdrum, so he set off to walk around Britain. I loved the impetuousness of his decision. He was enjoying the experience immensely, apart from some incidents with mud in Essex. I nodded at Moose, who had spread himself out on the rug at our feet; how was he managing, I asked? Chris stroked his stubble and explained: providing it was not too hot, Moose was in dog paradise, with new things to smell and chase every hour. We could have talked for hours, but unfortunately, I needed to catch the last bus back to my van.

The bus stop was half a mile away. It was 5.11 p.m. when I

left the Travelodge, and the bus was due to depart at 5.16 p.m. Just about possible, especially if the bus was late. I sprint-hobbled, slightly drunk. The route was tantalisingly straight, down into a valley and up the other side. I could see the bus. Tears of beer-fuelled hope welled in my eyes, replaced by tears of frustration as the bus drove off, a hundred yards away. No problem, expensive salvation was at hand via a nearby taxi. Perhaps that was the driver's strategy, waiting for people who miss the bus. With barely a word of introduction, 'Bert' launched into a story.

Bert was mid-50s, burly, cropped hair, and not a guy to argue with at the pub. Or anywhere else. Usually, I would chat about football or the local area – and avoid Brexit. But this man wanted to tell me about his transformed life. He glowed with excitement. Almost to the point where he drove a few extra miles to tell me the whole story. Perhaps he did, but no matter, I was as entranced as he was. He had flown with three friends to Thailand to play golf. Whilst in Bangkok, he logged onto his regular dating site; he had had no luck in Scarborough over the past twelve months. Perhaps this crowded, steamy city would offer better luck.

"Well lad, you wouldna believe it, but I couldna find a match for fifty mile," he grimaced.

I told him of an Airbnb host in Somerset, a woman younger than him, who had bemoaned the absence of unmarried, straight, younger-than-75 men within her radius.

"Gotta get outta yer comfort zone" stated Bert, grinning as he resumed.

To his surprise, in Bangkok, he met a woman on the site, originally from Kenya but living in Thailand, a senior expatriate employed at a global NGO. They met one afternoon at a coffee shop, moved a few yards to a restaurant, and then a nearby bar. Like the rest of the teeming city, they continued through much of the night. At 3am the woman asked: aren't you teeing off with your buddies in a few hours? Bert said he seized the moment – demonstrating the drama to me in the taxi by throwing both hands in the air. He asked his date a question straight out of a romcom script: would she spend the remainder of his holiday showing him Bangkok? To his delight she agreed and he jettisoned the golf and his buddies. After reconnecting his hands with the steering wheel, Bert asked me if I would like to see her picture. This was purely rhetorical. After some swerving, Google Maps was replaced by a photo of an attractive woman. Bert told me that they had enjoyed four days of bliss, exploring parts of Bangkok where few tourists ventured.

Now Bert had returned to Scarborough, navigating his taxi through the gales, and was busy planning the next few months. Based on her work travel, they had scheduled to meet in several places around the world. They had rendezvoused in Geneva; Nairobi was next. He could not stop grinning. The man was lost in love.

This had turned out to be a surprising day. First, a fellow walker had messaged me in the very hour when we each passing through Scarborough, and now here was Bert the Taxi sharing his love story. Both these guys had taken the initiative. I concluded that I should be more proactive. The year would be over in less than three months. What then? I headed south towards Hull, where I would be treated to a lesson in proactiveness.

CHAPTER 24

VISION AND ACTION

"Vision without action is merely a dream. Action without vision just passes the time. Vision with action can change the world." — Joel A. Barker.

Day 284, 26th March 2019, Hull, North Yorkshire, 3,231 miles

I knew by now that the stories were everywhere along the journey, lying like sea-carved driftwood tossed onto the beach. Nevertheless, even by the year's standards, our host in Hull, Simon, stood out. My friend Richard and I had arrived in Hull after a long day's walk along the Lincolnshire coast.

"Hello, now don't tell me, you're Laurence, and you must be Richard," beamed the jovial, bald man as we alighted from our van.

I thought Simon was in his early forties, although later, we learned he was a decade older. Simon guessed our names from the signs on my van. A few weeks earlier, my trusty Cancer Research UK partner, Jo, had produced several enormous magnetic photo-signs. I overcame my bashfulness about having my face plastered over the van when I realised the text donation number was a nice little earner. Random people would knock on the window and proffer a £20 note with a quick, "Good on yer, son." Simon was gesticulating us to walk inside..

"Come, see my lovely garden and meet my wife," he encouraged, holding open an immense, 15-foot wooden gate. "My lovely garden and even lovelier wife," Simon corrected himself. "Catherine."

The world changed, from a ramshackle street in a poor neighbourhood of Hull, to a sizable 17th-century garden, replete with arches and paths and box hedges and gracious tranquillity. We had emerged from the back of the wardrobe into Narnia! Simon led us along the gravel and brick paths, revelling in the statues under the arches, the four-lion-head fountain surrounded by a bed of herbs, and the newly planted espaliered fruit trees. He explained that each of the walled arches was slightly smaller than its neighbour, to enhance the sense of perspective when gazing down at the garden from the house. Astonishing. Who thinks like this?

A friendly-looking woman in her thirties was hanging up the laundry on a line in the garden, amiably chatting to her children, aged about six and four.

"Meet Catherine," grinned Simon. "These are the walkers," he said to her, nodding to us. Catherine smiled, but before she had a chance to speak, Simon continued.

"Guess how we met?" he asked Richard and me. Catherine looked a little wary or perhaps weary. This seemed like too much information too soon, but there was no escaping Simon's passion. We waited.

"Seven years ago, I was running a disability swimming club. Catherine joined one Saturday because she was teaching swimming at a special needs school. I was captivated. By the time Friday rolled around, I asked her to marry me!"

Richard and I raised our eyebrows at each other and then at Catherine to see whether Simon was joking. Catherine shook her head, smiling, and confirmed that it was true. Was every Airbnb guest treated to this origin story, I wondered?

"Not only that," explained Simon, "but I'd started renovating this house, so we slept in a tent in the garden for a few months and then the basement. Catherine was most understanding."

We were evidently staying with a crazily romantic, impetuous couple. Still, who was I to judge? A few months after meeting Melitta in Malawi, I had excitedly told her that my next job was on a Mediterranean island and asked her to join me. She shook her head with a grin, brushed her unruly curly hair back, and told me that St. Helena Island was in the middle of the Atlantic. But yes, she would still come. Meanwhile, Simon was describing the renovation.

Built in 1853 by a fishing magnate, by the early 2000s the house had fallen derelict and was scheduled to be demolished. Indeed, the town council had condemned the whole street. Simon, who ran a gardening business, spotted an opportunity. He asked the Council if they would sell him the dwelling. He promised to apply to the National Lottery Fund for a grant to renovate the five unoccupied flats, turning them back into a family home. He argued that this would help the Council to sell other properties on the street, and the neighbourhood might recover. He won the councillors over. The couple had renovated the property for the past seven years – Catherine worked as a teacher while Simon added plastering, joinery, and bricklaying to his gardening skills. In the last few months, they had started advertising rooms. Neighbours had copied Simon's idea, and the street was recovering.

Simon and Catherine had introduced some unusual features. The shower in Richard's room had a domed ceiling constructed from a plaster cast moulded around half an exercise ball. The lighting was provided by a round crystal disco ball, so a shower involved multi-coloured rays of light reflecting on the water droplets. Only the Bee Gees were missing, Richard said.

Simon's energy extended beyond the house and garden. He decided to restore a derelict Victorian street fountain, to revitalise civic pride and reinstate beauty to the neighbourhood. The town council told him there was no money and that old fountains were not a priority. Undaunted, Simon wrote a catchy song about being proud to live in Hull and offered to teach it at morning assemblies at nearby schools. The teachers loved him. Then he initiated a 'name-a-brick' scheme for brickwork around the proposed fountain. The students became excited, singing the song and asking their parents to chip in a brick. Local businesses provided materials and expertise. The councillors realised that the community was mobilising. Suddenly, fixing derelict fountains was a priority. The National Lottery chipped in. The neighbourhood celebrated the grand re-opening two years later. The councillors spoke eloquently about their vision for the community and the role of fountains in beautifying the streetscape. Credit splashed around as vigorously as the fountain's water, blessing everyone.

I marvelled at Simon's lobbying ingenuity. Were there lessons for me?

Originally, I thought that my walk might help husbands remind their wives about screening, but now I realised this was too ambitious – after all, the thought never crossed my mind with Melitta. But what about girls reminding their mothers?

Simon's house furnished the answer the next day, after Richard left at 5 a.m. to drive two hundred miles to arrive at work on time. Later that morning, in the breakfast room I was munching on toast and marmalade, peering through the window at the garden's arches in the garden, when a fellow guest wandered in. We shared a pot of tea and she shared her story.

'Sita' was an open-faced, smile-laden woman in her mid-forties, combining a business-like manner with an empathising tilt of the head. My toast grew cold as I listened.

"I worked for a publishing house, editing coffee table books. One day my mum called to say she'd been diagnosed with stage 4 lung cancer. I nursed her and decided there had to be more to life than picture books. I enrolled in a medical statistics degree. Now I'm running questionnaires with focus groups for the National Health Service."

"Wow, quite a change. What are you investigating?" I prompted.

"The NHS is always encouraging women to get screened for cervical cancer. They put up posters in doctors' waiting rooms, and now they advertise on the sides of buses and on TV, but they're not reaching some women. I'm studying women who attended screening after a break of at least six years, twice the recommended three-year frequency. What kept them from showing up before? And why did they suddenly decide to present themselves?"

"Good grief, that's incredible." The toast crumbs fell out of my seven-day stubble in surprise. "Let me tell you why I'm staying here." After I had recounted my tale, Sita brightened.

"I guess you'll be interested. I like the focus group format because it leads to a richer conversation. We have five to eight women, and the conversation typically lasts forty-five minutes. The ladies don't respond to the screening letter because they're busy, it's awkward, it hurt last time, or they're in a monogamous relationship, or they don't want a male doctor. But there's one reason why they change their mind."

"Let me guess," I interrupted. "I bet their teenage daughters remind them because now at school, they have the HPV vaccine, so they tell their mothers to be screened."

Seeing Sita's amused look, I tried again: "Maybe it's their friends?"

My companion grinned and shook her head.

"Great ideas," she smiled, "but I'm afraid not. The women had questions. But they were nervous to ask for the doctor's time. So, some doctors' practices asked the head nurse to call women who hadn't attended screening for several years and have a chat. It worked. Simple as that. A fifteen-minute chat, generally with a female nurse, to listen to their concerns, and they were often comfortable going ahead. Of course, this doesn't work for everyone – we're only interviewing women who returned to screening. But it was a consistent finding."

"Wow, that's cool," I drooled. "You must be delighted you left behind that whole coffee-table book gig."

"Mm-hmm," Sita agreed, glancing at her watch. "Gotta be off. Good luck with your walk. I've never met anyone doing that."

With that dollop of praise, she was gone. I felt educated and humbled. She had deliberately turned, mid-career, to find purpose. I was walking, which was fine but fleeting. I needed to leave something behind.

That morning I bid farewell to Simon, standing on the street. Recalling one of my minor obsessions, I mentioned that a few trees would make the road leafier. Simon knew that, but he graciously nodded. A few months later, he texted a photo of a planting ceremony on Coltman Street, Hull, with a local councillor. There was never any doubt.

Whether in the realm of romance – both Bert the Taxi and Simon – or restoring neighbourhoods, I was being treated to master classes in the fruits of proactively reaching out and taking risks. They showed their vulnerability by reaching out. They were comfortable with their own judgment about people. Their trust was repaid. And good things resulted. I began the walk down the long, flat Lincolnshire coast with plenty on my mind.

CHAPTER 25

JOY

"The soul's joy lies in doing." —Percy Bysshe Shelley.

Day 289, 31st March 2019, Mablethorpe, Lincolnshire, 3,258 miles

My friend Chris Wallisch had flown in from the US for a week of walking. Chris arrived with fine music, good humour, and a yearning to experience all things British. We diverted to Liverpool for two days to visit the Cavern Club before returning to the east coast. We turned up the music to full volume.

Chris and I had been friends for twenty years. He and his wife, Christine, lived a hundred yards up the road in Bethesda, Maryland. We both had three children, matched in age and gender. The kids had grown up together, as well as children from two other families on the same street, roaming and tumbling in and out of each other's houses. One frozen February day, fifteen years earlier, Chris had suggested running during Lent. Later this morphed into an annual tradition, which we called 5@5 – five miles at five a.m., every weekday of Lent, whatever the weather.

Lacking super-human levels of willpower, I knew I couldn't do that by myself. But with Chris waiting outside, there was no choice but to struggle out of bed, cursing the alarm.

I drove the van while Chris pointed out road signs with bafflement. The eyes of an outsider reveal the quirks of the English. What does 'No fly-tipping' mean, he asked. What are 'naked lights', and why are they prohibited in gas stations? George Bernard Shaw's quote about how England and America are two countries separated by the same language didn't seem to go far enough.

Chris's job was one we all wish we could tell our children when they ask, "Dad, what do you do?" Chris, who designed satellite launches, helped plan the NASA New Horizons probe, which flew by Pluto in July 2015. A week before the fly-by, the power system on the probe failed, and Chris' backup design kicked in, instructing the computer to re-boot. A long-distance version of the IT guy saying, "Switch it off and on again." It worked. Because of Chris' fail-safe design, mankind saw close-ups of Pluto for the first time.

Today was a bright March day, with the deep blue sky lifting our spirits. Chris and I were striding along the remote Lincolnshire coast, heading south from the hamlet of Saltfleet towards the seaside town of Mablethorpe. A stiff breeze carried our words away. The tide had retreated half a mile: endless, ridged sand melding with the sea and sky. Bright blue jellyfish lay dotted around sporadically on the drying sand, plotting their next victim.

"Whoa, what do you think that is?" asked Chris, pointing seawards.

Like a scene out of a movie, a galloping horse appeared on the horizon at the sea's edge. Back and forth along the beach, hooves barely touching the ground, almost flying, with grace and abandon, a trail of spray gusting behind, the pink-jacketed rider crouched low in the saddle. We started walking towards the surf line, hoping to intersect with them. Nearer the sea, we spotted a man and a woman with a long-lensed camera.

"Perhaps they're filming something," I ventured.

No one else was in sight. We strolled faster towards the sea, determined to arrive before they left. Eventually, the rider, a girl aged around thirteen, spotted us and wheeled around. We intersected with the cameraman, her grandfather, and his wife. The horse and girl were breathless with excitement, savouring the wind, waves, and expanse of beach. The bright spring sunlight accentuated the contrasts between the horse's cocoa-brown coat, the arctic-blue sky, and the girl's watermelon-pink coat. It was infectious – we all beamed as we chatted. Even the horse's sweat-heavy breathing conveyed rapture.

Untrammelled joy is infectious and a little envy-inducing. Like when you're waiting to meet someone at the airport, and the person next to you hurls themselves with a shriek into the arms of the arriving traveller. You can't help smiling – and wondering when that last happened to you.

"This horse, Ruby, was destined for the knacker's yard. We knew our granddaughter was keen on riding, so we bought her. Our granddaughter learned to ride on Ruby. Now she loves galloping along the beach, as you can see. Ruby likes it too," the man explained to Chris and me.

"Imagine, Ruby would've been horsemeat. We couldn't let that happen. But what brings you two out here?" added the woman.

However, the girl and the horse were impatient. Enough of the chit-chat. Off they galloped, fading into the distance, into the spray of the surf, and our hearts sang. I wished I, too, could ride and experience the salty spray in my face on a spring day on a Lincolnshire beach.

That afternoon, after five hours and ten miles of sandy

171

beach and wind-blown conversation, Chris and I arrived at the faded seaside resort of Mablethorpe. Chris set about photographing the rock shops, the ice cream vendors, and one-arm bandit emporia. It was 3:45 p.m. on a Sunday, and we were ready for refreshment. But first, we needed to arrange transport back to our starting point, a tiny hamlet a few miles up the Lincolnshire coast. No buses ran on Sundays, and Mablethorpe had no train station, so a taxi was the only option. We ordered enormous sausage rolls and steaming cups of strong tea. The waitress in the café kindly wrote down three taxi numbers, and I started calling.

"Hello, any chance of a taxi back up the coast to Saltfleet?" I asked.

"Sorry mate, our drivers finish at four on Sundays, and that journey would go over the time limit," the dispatcher replied.

"Well, would any driver like to earn a bit more if I add extra to the fare?" I suggested.

"Nah, they've got stuff to do," he replied.

OK. I wondered what happened at 4 p.m. in Mablethorpe that was so interesting, but never mind. Onto the next number.

"I've only got one taxi," he answered after I'd made my request.

"That's OK. My friend and I just need one taxi to get to Saltfleet." I shook my head in bewilderment.

"No can do, son. Gotta stay here in case someone wants a taxi."

I was gobsmacked. "That's us, we're in Mablethorpe, we need a taxi, and we're ready to pay a good fare to be taken back to our vehicle," I said.

He suggested another service – which happened to be the third number on my list. Astonishingly, the third taxi driver also said he only had one vehicle. I told him that one taxi was already waiting in Mablethorpe. But he wasn't prepared to negotiate.

This was truly bleak. We couldn't trudge back along the beach for four hours. Searching for plan B, I asked the café's server if we could pay anyone to drive us back after their shift. No, they had hours to work. But, she suggested, why don't you pop around the corner and talk to the taxi company in person? I was doubtful; I'd just called them. I plodded over, heavy-hearted, and spoke to the dispatcher. She wasn't the person who'd answered the phone before. Suddenly, the afternoon lit up: of course, it was on her way home, could we wait while she found her husband and son? Salvation! I nonchalantly told Chris it was all sorted. Melitta's spirit at work again, I presumed.

Twenty minutes later, we were swaying in the back of the taxi, chatting to the dispatcher's eleven-year-old son. He told us that times were hard because there weren't enough customers in Mablethorpe. Somewhat at odds with our experience that afternoon! He explained that his dad was usually the driver, while his mum did the dispatching. We held onto the straps and wondered why his mum was driving now. She employed the straight-line method, smoothing out the bends at speed. I hoped that no one else was doing the same in the other direction. The van had an intercom system, which wasn't switched on, so his parents sitting up front couldn't hear our conversation. We asked the boy why his mother didn't drive for the taxi company. He gazed at us solemnly.

"My mum gets road rage."

When we stepped out of the taxi, we thanked our driver sincerely, full of the joy of still being alive. That evening our host, the manager of a pub, served up a home-cooked pheasant pie. As we supped her ale, she told us how she had plucked the pheasants and extracted the birdshot. Chris nodded. Now he understood how the Brits lived: walking around in shorts in winter, riding horses on the beach, hanging on in taxis driving Formula One style, washing pheasant pie down with warm ale, avoiding naked lights and piling builders' rubble next to no fly-tipping signs. A few days later he headed home to the States, and I entered the most solitary part of the walk.

THE WASH

APRIL 2, 2019 – APRIL 15, 2019,
139 MILES, 599 FEET OF CLIMB

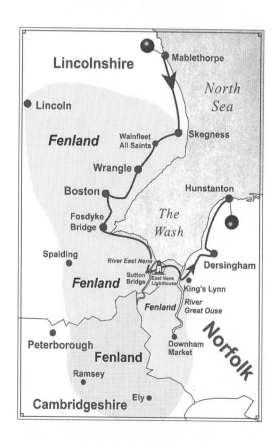

CHAPTER 26

SOLITUDE

"Nature does not hurry, yet everything is accomplished." — Lao Tzu.

Day 299, 10th April 2019, Sutton Bridge, Lincolnshire, 3,370 miles

About of solitude, plus an unanticipated discovery, led to a resolution. It started on the grassy sea walls of southern Lincolnshire, a place to empty one's mind and fill one's lungs. Aching miles of tufted grass sea walls stretched out endlessly, fading into a hazy, blue-grey tapestry of sea, sky, and land. The expanse of mudflats, sandbanks, and salt marshes was soothing, almost hypnotic. A rich cornucopia of wintering and migrant birds feasted on the land. Melitta would have recognised the dunlin, grey plover, knot, and oystercatcher, all hungrily devouring the mud-dwelling invertebrates. Sadly, I had failed to master the names of birds and trees, defeated by procrastination and socialising. Still, I was mesmerised by their sounds: the arching shrieks of the seagulls trailing in the wind, the mournful honking of the geese, and the contented tweeting of the waders as they spotted another delicacy. Nature was busy; I was an interloper.

Hours passed over long, solitary days. Time slowed, matching my decreased pace in the long grass atop the earthen sea walls. This was the first occasion during the year I had spent so much time with just myself. I thought and thought, ideas bumping into each other like new skaters on an ice rink. After two days I concluded within that I was not hermit material. I could only take so much of my own company. But buried beneath this simple learning, I did have one thought. Something about the outcome of suffering. I did not subscribe to the view that 'what does not kill you makes you stronger,' when dealing with personal tragedy. I did believe that enduring pain helped to build empathy. But this walk had added an extra dimension. Because I was meeting so many people, often in their homes, I was being treated to a deluge of intimate personal stories. I witnessed people all along the response-to-suffering spectrum, from those who sat in their armchairs all day, enduring life by television, through to energetic individuals campaigning for change. Most people muddled along somewhere between, slipping in an extra kindness among the daily chores. I was being treated to a masterclass in inspiration, each experience another dab of colour on an impressionist painting.

One blue-skied, windy April day I traipsed along the endless green sea wall, picking my way through knee-high spring grass. I experimented with walking at the landward base of the mound, hoping to find shorter grass and shelter from the wind. A few minutes later, after plunging a foot into a pool of dark, brackish water camouflaged as meadow, I stumbled back to the top, holding my cap firmly to my head, muttering obscenities. Then, without warning or expectation, I came upon a lighthouse.

There was no access to the stark white building before me; it was in private hands and for sale. The extraordinary story of its one-time inhabitant was briefly sketched in broad strokes on a noticeboard outside.

This lonely building, the East Nene lighthouse, miles from everywhere, was home in the 1930s to an unusual man: Peter Scott, son of Robert Scott, who perished on his journey back from the South Pole, and godson to J.M. Barrie, author of Peter Pan. In 1933 Peter, aged 24, was washed ashore from his sailboat near the lighthouse. Captivated by the building and unsure what to do with his life, he moved there for six years, becoming a wildlife artist and writer.

I stood there for thirty minutes, caught up in a mélange of senses – listening to the wind carrying the geese's melancholy cry, inhaling the marsh's salty odours, and absorbing the visceral solitude.

Scott's six years of contemplation in the wild – together with his painting, writing, and design – led him later to found the World Wildlife Fund. At a lesser scale, I ruminated on my little effort. I was shortcutting the time: one year instead of six. I lacked any ability to paint or design. Hmm, that only left writing. I resolved then to document the walk to keep the journey alive and feel less alone.

EAST ANGLIA

APRIL 16, 2019 – MAY 13, 2019
276 MILES, 6,845 FEET OF CLIMB

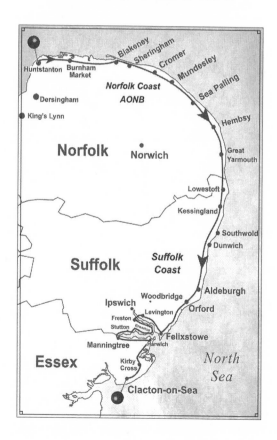

CHAPTER 27

TELLING THE STORY

*"What's the story of the hidden daisies among the roses,
and the stars which break at the dawn,
or the littered leaves after the storm.
Unsung"* — Saleem Sharma.

Day 330, 11th May 2019, Erwarton, Suffolk, 3,698 miles

In Suffolk for a few days in May, my friend Paula joined me. Paula and I first met in 1983 when I moved into a two-story apartment block in Gaborone, Botswana. Gaborone was a sleepy little town in those days. The beating, dry heat would hang heavy on Sunday afternoons, to be whiled away at a *braai* (barbecue) with friends, although the occasional presence of Hugh Masekela playing at the local jazz bar livened life up. Paula, a dark-haired, thoughtful, feisty, and cheerful South African woman, lived quietly in the flat above. Sometimes we would share a cold beer and exchange notes on books. We both attended classes in the local language, Setswana – unfortunately, these had little effect on me. I left Botswana after three years, but we kept in touch. After apartheid ended, Paula returned to South Africa.

I felt honoured that she flew to the UK to join the walk.

Paula had had a life rich in rising to challenges, first as a student leader, standing up to the apartheid government; as a single mother raising her son in Botswana, the UK, and South Africa; as a professor rising to Dean of the Humanities faculty, and as a woman who faced her own severe scare with cervical cancer.

Paula and I stayed in a farmhouse in Erwarton, a village of 110 souls on the Shotley peninsula. A tranquil place with two surprising claims to fame. First, it was the last place in England to suffer an outbreak of the bubonic plague, in the early twentieth century. Twenty-two people were infected, of whom sixteen died.

We discovered the hamlet's second secret late on a golden-hued, spring afternoon at Erwarton's 13th-century church, St. Mary's. It was here, enveloped by the aroma of freshly mown grass, that we stumbled upon Anne Boleyn's heart!

Poor Anne, before her head was chopped off, had asked that her heart be returned to Erwarton, where she had played as a child at her uncle's manor house. There was the church, bereft of people, a little dusty, a field away. Anne's heart was buried under the organ, the tattered sign announced. It seemed so ineffably sad, imagining her cavorting around the grounds as a lively ten-year-old with no inkling of the palace intrigue to come.

One thing led to another and soon Paula and I were chatting about unearthing other choice tales. I had recently learned the story of how the Human Papilloma Virus (HPV) vaccine was discovered. In 1974 a German researcher named Harald zur Hausen postulated at a conference that cervical cancer was caused by HPV, a group of viruses common in humans. The conference attendees listened in silence, believing instead that cervical cancer was linked to the herpes virus. After doggedly pursuing the hypothesis for several years, zur Hausen showed that one virus type – HPV 16 – was present in around half of cervical cancer biopsies. Then his research team found that HPV 18 accounted for a further twenty per cent of cervical cancers. With these results, in 1984, zur Hausen proposed to several German pharmaceutical companies that they develop a vaccine. Bizarrely, they decided that the market was too small. Whoever made that decision should join the publishers who rejected the first Harry Potter book in the club of costly misjudgements. The rest of the 1980s passed and millions more women died of cervical cancer, but luckily the story was not over because a young Scottish researcher living in Australia, Dr Ian Frazer, had been inspired by zur Hausen's work. Frazer partnered with a Chinese scientist, Jian Zhou, at the University of Queensland and finally presented the first HPV vaccine to the scientific community in 1991. After seven more years of testing, human clinical trials began with two major pharmaceutical companies, Merck and GSK. Finally, in 2006, thirty-two years after Dr zur Hausen's silently received speech, trials showed that the vaccine provided almost 100% protection against HPV 16 and 18, and it was approved for use by Australia and the USA, followed by eighty more countries the following year. Dr zur Hausen was awarded the Nobel Prize for Medicine in 2008.

As we strolled through the warm May sunshine and budding fields, Paula told me what she had been doing recently. At the request of a South African philanthropist, she was interviewing people who were originally in the resistance movement, specifically to create an oral history archive of the people banned by the then apartheid government under the Suppression of Communism/Internal Security Acts. The plan was to place the recorded interviews into an archive. Paula was seeking out those who were less prominent, often women living in remote rural areas.

"We've identified about three hundred people but have only tracked down around half of them. Lots have died, or we couldn't trace them. Still, the interviews are going well. Guess the most interesting thing?" she asked.

I had no idea.

"They are amazed to be asked. Mostly, they've been living quietly for decades. Many became emotional, knowing they would have a voice and their memories would be recorded. Person after person has thanked us for reaching out, to hear their stories." Paula spoke quietly.

A mayfly perched on a blade of grass, and a Painted Lady butterfly hovered skittishly over a bud until our shadows fell upon them. Goosebumps pricked my skin in the silence as I listened to Paula's words. There are no heroes if no one knows; only heroic actions remembered but not acknowledged, like the proverbial tree falling in the forest. And then, after a few years, gone forever.

The encounter a few weeks earlier with Scott's lighthouse had left a strong impression on me. I had resolved then – very late – to document the walk. But it was Paula's anecdote that finally brought home to me the value of writing stories down. I had met dozens of ordinary-yet-extraordinary people over the year. I had to bring their stories to life: to see Anne Boleyn as a carefree girl playing in the fields instead of just the doomed second wife of Henry VIII.

I had six weeks to go. Some things were clear: I would write the walk up, focusing on the stories of those I had met. Listening to a mosaic of experiences, from quiet suffering to inspirational activity, had changed my outlook, lifting my gaze from downwards and rearwards, to the future.

ESSEX AND NORTH KENT

MAY 13, 2019 – JUNE 11, 2019
495 MILES, 8,107 FEET OF CLIMB

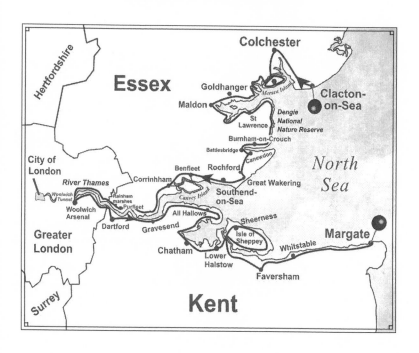

CHAPTER 28

GENERATIONAL CHANGE

"The greatest discovery of my generation is that a human being can alter his life by altering his attitudes." — William James.

Day 352, 2nd June 2019, Rainham Marshes, Essex, 4,035 miles

The dragonflies flitted among the long grasses, their iridescent flashes bestowing a glamorous sheen to the warm May morning. I stopped and listened, wishing I could differentiate between the calls of the birds serenading the day.

I was on the home stretch. I had called my children to say that the last day would be 23rd June, back into Seaford. There was the Thames estuary, Kent and a few miles in East Sussex left, with three weeks to go. But what lay ahead, beyond the path? Sometimes I woke in the early hours, sensing that the answer had arrived in a dream, striving to recall it, like trying to photograph a butterfly that won't rest on a leaf.

The ancient marshland adjoining the north bank of the Thames reeks of history, nature, and sometimes the effluent of Essex man. In medieval times, the monks of Lesnes Abbey grazed their sheep on the marshes. An inn, *The Three Crowns*, was built in the 1500s to serve passengers crossing the river, including pilgrims heading for Canterbury. However, by the late nineteenth century, wharves and industrial buildings had sprawled along Ferry Lane. Nature retreated. In 1906 the Ministry of Defence commandeered the land for a firing range. I knew nothing of this as I sauntered along the marshland, marvelling at the contrast between the egrets contentedly pulling worms from the mud and the modern industrial landscape a few hundred yards away, exemplified by the Queen Elizabeth Bridge. My feet felt light, buoyed by nature's resilience on the doorstep of industrial dockland London, when I suddenly came upon an unusual building set in the marshes: the visitor centre for the Royal Society for the Protection of Birds.

The RSPB bought Rainham Marshes from the Ministry of Defence in 2000, cleared the military ordnance, and restored the wetlands to their original state. The medieval sheep of Lesnes Abbey would recognise the landscape again. Over 280 species of birds have been spotted there, plus 33 types of butterflies. I resumed my stroll, listening to the birdsong, overlain by the distant hum of the vehicles crossing the Thames, thinking about societal change. Every generation shakes its head at the cruelties and ignorance of its predecessors. Today we wonder why people shot birds for pleasure, killed them for their feathers, and stole their eggs, almost to extinction? But the metamorphosis was sluggish: it took three generations of RSPB advocacy for the community to change its collective mind. I mused about my quest. Could cervical cancer really be eliminated in one generation?

Scrolling through my phone, it turned out that there was some positive news. A behavioural psychologist active in cervical cancer screening, Dr Rebecca Richards, had recently published some guest blogs on my website, mentioning how HPV infections fell by 86% in English women aged 16-21 who were eligible for the vaccine as teenagers between 2010 and 2016. The public health minister announced that the HPV vaccine would include boys aged 12-13 in England. *The Lancet* projected that Australia was set to eliminate cervical cancer by 2035. And the World Health Organisation had issued a call for global action to eliminate cervical cancer.

I crossed under the Thames through the Woolwich Foot Tunnel, a little-known gem. As I emerged, I passed by the coal jetty for the former Woolwich power station, which had belched out the residues from burning a thousand tons of coal daily from 1893 to 1978. Melitta had suffered from asthma since adolescence because she walked a mile to school along a busy London road, inhaling coal dust and diesel particles. After involuntarily gulping down gobfuls of truck emissions during the year, I felt what she had experienced. The electric vehicle revolution couldn't come too soon. Today the site serves as the car park for a leisure centre, which seems to be an improvement.

I glanced behind me, as the setting sun dipped beneath the waters of the River Thames. The City skyscrapers morphed into silhouettes. The river flowed languidly, lapping at the stanchions of the Victorian coal dock. I heard a fish splash in the river and was reminded that the Thames is the cleanest it has been for two hundred years, after being declared biologically dead in the 1950s. Reassured, I smiled to myself as I climbed back into the van. The WHO call to end cervical cancer was a game-changer. I was lucky to be riding a wave of change. Change within a generation.

SOUTH KENT AND EAST SUSSEX

JUNE 11, 2019 – JUNE 23, 2019
115 MILES, 5,212 FEET OF CLIMB

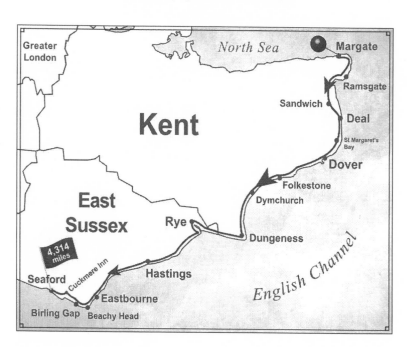

CHAPTER 29

ALMOST FULL CIRCLE

"You just stay the course, and do what it is that you do, and grow while you're doing it. Eventually, it will either come full circle, or at least you'll go to bed at night happy." — Jon Bon Jovi.

Day 366, 16th June 2019, Dungeness, Kent, 4,235 miles

I spent a day accompanied by Helen, one of Melitta's closest friends. We walked out along Romney marsh to the remote Dungeness headland, which was strangely fitting. Helen and her husband had lived nearby in the early 2000s when she and Melitta became close. They had returned to the UK, but we kept in touch, and Helen flew over to spend a week with Melitta shortly before she died. The two women had sat in Melitta's beloved garden, reminiscing, laughing, and crying, while Helen designed Melitta's rock garden. Seeing them saying their final goodbyes over those muggy August days in 2015 was heartbreaking and elating.

Now, nearly four years later, Helen was unchanged – a busy mother and teacher, passionate about injustice, funny, interesting, and one of the kindest people I knew. We chatted away happily as we trod along miles of shingle interspersed with clumps of desert-like vegetation. As we approached Dungeness Point, Helen pointed excitedly to a beach house.

"Oh my God, that's Prospect Cottage. The garden which Derek Jarmin built."

The late filmmaker had created an oasis of drought and salt-tolerant plants such as sea kale, wild carrot, lavender, sempervivum, heather, and cistus – as Helen told me, I didn't know the names – mixed in with artistically placed driftwood, cast iron, and old chains. There was no fence, so we picked our way among the plants, crunching on the beach gravel, as Helen rhapsodised about those last few bittersweet days with Melitta. The lonely aspect, gentle sea breeze, salty air, thriving plants, the memory-infused atmosphere, Helen's enthusiasm. . .it felt right.

That evening, I thought more about Helen and her visit to Melitta in August 2015. And, suddenly, in a moment so ordinary I remember no details, in the unfathomable way that our brains work, the revelation arrived.

And it was the surprisingly social nature of the year which yielded the insight. It wasn't about cervical cancer, awareness-raising, or changing behaviour. Or about walking or recovering from grief. Or about me.

Born from Helen's actions, from the 82-year-old woman walking the South West Coast Path for her granddaughters, from Dee Cartledge and her foundation, and from the dozens of friends and relatives who had joined me through the year.

It was simply:

What can we do for those we love?

Now, before it's too late. Because, as we know, our lives can change in a moment.

A universal question that we all answer in our own way. It had taken almost the whole year for me to understand. Who knows, perhaps Melitta's spirit felt that I needed a nudge to stumble upon the answer before reaching the end.

The next morning I was relaxing in the garden of my Airbnb with a mug of tea and a digestive biscuit. A jumble of pink roses and peonies jostled for space in a flower bed a few feet away. I savoured the moment of relaxation and opened my emails. There was one from someone I did not know. A librarian from near my home in Bethesda wrote that she was clearing up magazines which had been left out by the patrons that day. She idly leafed through a months-old copies of a local magazine when she saw a feature article about my walk. The story resonated with her; she too had suffered a loss when her husband had died of leukaemia a few years earlier. She wrote that she was not sure how I would take an unsolicited email, but that if I did read it, would I like to stroll along the local C&O canal and sip a beer afterwards. I called my emotional adviser again, my elder daughter, Emily.

"Do what you think feels right," was her sage advice. Wasn't that the third time she had said that?

I replied to the email, saying yes, I'd be delighted. Her initiative reminded me of others I had witnessed: the man in Cornwall offering to renovate his date's house, Bert the taxi driver abandoning his golf buddies in Bangkok after talking through the night, Simon asking his swimming instructor to marry him after a week, Ruth heading out to Vietnam to teach English and meeting the love of her life. The least I could do was to respond to the courage of someone taking such a vulnerable risk.

CHAPTER 30

LAST DAY

"The tragedy of life doesn't lie in not reaching your goal. The tragedy lies in having no goals to reach." — Benjamin E. Mays.

Day 373, 23rd June 2019, Seaford, East Sussex, 4,295 miles

The year was over all too quickly. The final walk wound 3.7 miles along the bucolic valley of Cuckmere Haven, up to Seaford Head for a view of the Seven Sisters and then descended into Seaford, arriving back at the Martello Tower one year and seven days after starting. Over thirty people joined, while more headed straight to the pub. Spirits were jovial, and the view of the Seven Sisters was magnificent. Jo from CRUK laughed that, yet again, I had chosen a hilly route for her.

My mother beamed from her wheelchair at the finish line. After hugging Emily, Nic and Georgie, and noting that the wind was not bad, she asked:

"Well, Laurence, that was a fine walk. What are you going to do now?"

Hmm, I had no answer to that.

What had I learned?

The physical journey was relatively easy, buttressed by purpose, support from friends and strangers, and CRUK. I witnessed that behind the blithe phrase "the kindness of strangers", there lies a deep well of human generosity. I grew to empathise with people living in remote communities, left bereft as their bus timetables shrank.

The salving power of the outdoors and nature's vulnerability and resilience were reinforced daily. Gazing out across blustery waves on a winter's day, waiting for a grasshopper to jump, listening to an oystercatcher's trilling, lying in a meadow smelling the grass, tasting salty air on a windswept beach, inhaling the aroma of a forest path. . . the list is as endless as my hunger for these experiences.

I saw many striving to overcome loneliness and was reminded that simply listening helps. I was treated to a course about the depth of enduring friendships. Richard texted bad jokes every day through the year and walked frequently. Friends flew in from all over the globe to join. Despite not being there in person, Melitta attracted people to walk throughout the year. Innumerable conversations revolve around what she would have said.

I was surprised to learn how many people have been touched by cervical cancer, either through a lucky escape or a personal tragedy. I was reminded of the huge impact of women dying of a preventable disease in the prime of life. Whole families are wrecked.

In addition, however, the year left me with a feeling that there was more, beyond the boundaries of the rational. The coincidences, the unexpected connections, the gorse bush's roots holding when I grabbed it to stop sliding down a steep slope into the sea. . . I felt that Melitta's spirit was there too. My role was to enable connections, to prise stories out as carefully as on an archaeological dig and share them.

At the party afterward, my younger daughter Georgie produced home-baked carrot cake and a tray of cookies decorated with a map of the walk. Melitta, who always baked a special cake for everyone's birthday, would have been proud.

Many years earlier, on a road trip with Emily, Nic, and Georgie, Melitta and I were being buffeted by the familiar cries of "when will we be there?" In a vain attempt to inject mystery, we announced that we were "going somewhere we've never been before." Gradually the phrase became embedded in the family. The journey around England and Wales took me somewhere I had never been before, with three revelations. The first was practical: listen, and then tell good stories, which will help with outreach. Second, and more personal: I was ready to learn to love again. I was sure that Melitta's spirit had helped me reach this understanding. And finally, there was the revelation-question:

What can we do for those we love?

Now, before it is too late. Because our lives can change in a moment.

EPILOGUE

A few days after the end of the walk, back in Bethesda, I met the courageous librarian. We walked along the canal, laughed, and enjoyed a beer afterwards. She smacked her lips with unadulterated pleasure as she took the first sip. Here was a woman who enjoyed life and books and walking and people. I was smitten.

The year enabled me to harvest stories which would otherwise have lain untouched, like ripe apples lying in an orchard. These pages allowed me to pick them up and polish them a tad, as my attempt to transform the one-year trek to something longer-lasting. This book became an extension of that journey. A reminder that no person should lose a mother, daughter, sister, wife, partner, or friend to cervical cancer.

Two years after the walk ended, I heard from Frederike, who walked Hadrian's Wall with her husband Bas and me. She said a friend had probably been saved by our campaign. After she told her book club about why she and Bas walked, her friend scheduled a check-up. They found stage 1 cervical cancer, which was treated successfully.

On 15 November 2023 England's National Health Service

announced that it was aiming to eliminate cervical cancer by 2040. England is one of the first countries in the world to set such a target.

ACKNOWLEDGMENTS

I would like to thank Cancer Research UK for their partnership during the walk, especially Jo Marriott, as well as Alex Horne, Becky Trout, Catherine Deans, Ellie Dixon-Smith, Heidi Connell, Laura Holland, Philippa Hurst, Simon Ledsham, Sophie Barber, Tom Lay, and Trudy Stammer,

Vanda Gajic designed and managed the walk's website (www.3500toendit.com). Jackie Barber's contribution as publicist was invaluable. Emily Carter created the logo, t-shirts and stickers and narrated a short video which was viewed over 600,000 times. Georgie Carter baked the end-of-walk cake and cookies and organised a wonderful set of haiku from the walkers. Nic Carter set up a bitcoin account for donations and encouraged his crypto friends to contribute. Stephen Carter provided a base for R&R and hosted the end-of-walk party. Sasha Aleston and Max Fong decorated the van. Rebecca Richards wrote several important blogs about cervical cancer screening for my website.

I am grateful for everyone who joined the walk, including Alex Tarrant-Anderson, Alia Diamond, Ana Gunther, Andrea Lewis, Andrew Donaldson, Andrew Gunther, Arezo Kohistany, Ariana Mavaddat, Auzi Knippenberg, Bas Mohrmann, Bayo Oyewole, Becky Trout, Bethan Toner, Bruce Gailey, Catherine

Deans, Chris Thompson, Chris Wallisch, Dan Wotton, David Crush, David Donaldson, Debbie Fantom, Elan Cusiac-Barr, Elizabeth Donaldson, Elizabeth Donaldson's friend, Emily Carter, Emmanuel Nyirinkindi, Esther Varkay, Fiona Chesterman, Freddie Lister, Frederike Mohrmann, Funke Oyewole, Gareth Smyth, Georgie Carter, Hannah McClelland, Heidi Connell, Helen Featherstone, Helena Mathieson, Ian Mathieson, Jackie Barber, Jacob Lister, Jan Rose, Jan Woodhouse Pickton, Jide, Joanna Wardlaw, John Kjorstad, Julia Carter, Julia Gunther, Julian Borrill, Helen Nichol, James Close, Jo Marriott, Karen Campbell-Mathieson, Kristin Brady, Lada Strelkova, Lalage Clay, Laura Holland, Lee Moersen, Lena Enzminger, Liam Jenkins, Lisa Daniel, Loti Irwin, Luke Tetley, Marta Moersen, Melissa Daniel, Monica Altamirano, Muneer Ferozie, Natasha Jessen-Petersen, Neil Fantom, Nettie Alevropoulos-Borrill, Nic Carter, Nik Wotton, Pat, Paul Da Rita, Paula Ensor, Pepijn de Jong, Peter Enzminger, Philip Bath, Philip Lister, Philippa Hurst, Phyllis, Richard Boulter, Richard Wotton, Sara Clancy, Sasha Aleston, Sheila, Simon Ledsham, Sophie Barber, Sophie Voruna, Stephen Bath, Stephen Carter, Stephen Lister, Sujata Lamba, Tanya Alevropoulos, Tasha Alevropoulos-Borrill, Thomas Maier, Tim Daniel, Tom Lay, Tony Odone, Trudy Stammer, Vanda Gajic, Vicky Wotton and Wendy England. There were quite a few others, and I know I will (rightly) get into trouble for my forgetfulness.

I am delighted that my mother, Barbara Carter, was able to wave me off at the start and welcome me back a year later, at Seaford's Martello Tower.

Writing this book proved far more challenging than the walk! Nicola Perry's excellent guidance helped me to finalize the manuscript. I would like to thank my writing group: Gina Hagler, as our teacher and guide, and Alan Miller, Jorge Goldstein, John Hasse, and Peter Eisner, for their terrific insights and honest feedback. I would also like to thank other relatives and friends who read the manuscript: Andy Gunther, Chris Wallisch, David Donaldson, Emily Carter, Georgie Carter, Julian Borrill, Lee Moersen, Marta Moersen, Nic Carter, Noel Gunther, Sasha Aleston, Sonha Mason, Stephen Carter and Tanya Alevropoulos.

I also benefited from participating for a year in another writing group. Thank you, Pamela Toutant, as leader, together with Ursula Werner, Lisa Johnson, Anne Newman, Betsy Palmer, Maude Fish, Dianne Neiman, and Fernando Manibog.

My children, Emily, Nic, and Georgie Carter have been endlessly patient and encouraging as I have meandered slowly along the writing journey. And, above all, a special thank you to Sonha Mason, for your optimism and guidance, and belief. I simply would not have completed this manuscript without you.

Finally, a word about the wonderful non-profit which supported Melitta after her diagnosis. Hope Connections for Cancer Support offers free services to help people with cancer and their loved ones deal with the emotional and physical impact of cancer. They offer a wide range of professionally facilitated programs of emotional support, education, wellness, and hope. Programs include support groups, exercise classes, and other activities that combat depression and stress and provide a caring community to ensure patient outcomes are improved. They are located in Maryland but also offer their services virtually. They are dedicated to making sure that no one has to face cancer alone. HopeConnectionsForCancer.org

Made in the USA
Middletown, DE
01 October 2024

61723583R00123